BREWERS ASSOCIATION

# DRAUGHT BEER QUALITY MANUAL

FOURTH EDITION

Prepared by the Technical Committee
of the Brewers Association

Brewers Publications®
A Division of the Brewers Association
PO Box 1679, Boulder, Colorado 80306-1679
BrewersAssociation.org
BrewersPublications.com

© Copyright 2019 by Brewers Association℠

All rights reserved. No portion of this book may be reproduced in any form without written permission of the publisher. Neither the authors, editors, nor the publisher assume any responsibility for the use or misuse of information contained in this book.

Proudly printed in the United States of America.

10 9 8 7 6 5 4 3 2 1
ISBN-13: 978-1-938469-60-2
Library of Congress Cataloging-in-Publication Data

Names: Brewers Association.
Title: Draught beer quality manual / prepared by the Technical Committee of the Brewers Association.
Description: Fourth edition. | Boulder, Colorado : Brewers Publications, a Division of the Brewers Association, [2019] | Includes bibliographical references and index.
Identifiers: LCCN 2018045113 (print) | LCCN 2018046073 (ebook) | ISBN 9781938469619 (E-book) | ISBN 9781938469602
Subjects: LCSH: Brewing--Handbooks, manuals, etc. | Beer--Handbooks, manuals, etc. | Brewing--Equipment and supplies. | Brewing industry--United States.
Classification: LCC TP577 (ebook) | LCC TP577 .D73 2019 (print) | DDC 663/.3--dc23
LC record available at https://lccn.loc.gov/2018045113

Publisher: Kristi Switzer
Technical Editor: Ernie Jimenez
Copyediting: Iain Cox
Proofreading: Iain Cox
Indexing: Doug Easton
Art Direction, Cover, and Interior Design: Jason Smith
Production: Justin Petersen
Cover Photo: Luke Trautwein

# TABLE OF CONTENTS



Photo © Christine Celmins Photography

# PREFACE

I am honored to be writing the preface to this, the fourth edition of the Brewers Association *Draught Beer Quality Manual*, on behalf of the Draught Beer Quality subcommittee. I am a bit of a pack rat with my emails, but it is times like this when I appreciate my e-hoarder tendencies. I have enjoyed looking back at early communications about the development of this manual. In doing so, I was reminded of all of the amazing contributions that have come from this group over the years. I want to take this opportunity to highlight the evolution of this group, as well as capture a brief history of accomplishments.

I was privileged to be asked by Kim Jordan to join this small working group at its inception in 2007. The group, led by Ken Grossman of Sierra Nevada, consisted of only a handful of craft brewers tasked with improving the quality of draught beer at retail. As I look back at the original correspondence, words like "pamphlet" and "handbook" were used to describe the original scope. As we began to collaborate, we quickly realized the scope of the project was going to be much larger.

Right away, this small group knew it would be essential to include the industry's large brewers. If the mission was to create a set of industry-wide recommendations, it was imperative we had both the buy-in and the vast knowledge of the large US brewers. This was not only a chance to align the beer industry, but a wonderful opportunity to merge a collective knowledge. Within months a diverse group was assembled, including representatives from the Brewers Association, Boulevard, Coors, Gambrinus, InBev International, Miller, New Belgium, Sierra Nevada, and Upstream.

During its first year, the group maintained an energetic pace, holding countless phone meetings and also two conferences, during which the entire group traveled to Chicago and Denver to collaborate in person. By April of 2009 the group had released an initial set of recommendations published in wiki format. The group immediately began presenting the compiled recommendations at industry conferences and guild meetings to gather feedback. Once the final content had been assembled, the group worked with Ray Daniels of Cicerone® to bring to life the first edition of the *Draught Beer Quality Manual*, published in August of 2009.

Photo © Getty/Zdenko_Simekovic

To date, the working group, now a subcommittee as of December 2013, has published four editions of the *Draught Beer Quality Manual* (including this one), the versatile *Draught Beer Quality for Retailers*, and six educational fact sheets; the subcommittee also maintains an interactive microsite on https://www.BrewersAssociation.org to support the ever-growing library of material relating to draught quality. In addition, since 2011, the subcommittee has hosted the annual Draught Beer Quality Summit, held in conjunction with the Great American Beer Festival® in Denver.

The Draught Beer Quality subcommittee continues to grow and evolve to remain the definitive resource on draught quality for the US beer market. On the next page, you will see acknowledgements listing current and historical contributors. Without these extremely knowledgeable and passionate volunteers, this manual, and all the accomplishments of this group, would not be possible. This group continues to challenge itself to deliver draught beer in the way the brewer intended and in a way that surpasses the expectations of our shared consumers. ■

**Matt Meadows**
*Brewers Association Draught Beer Quality Subcommittee Chair*
Director of Field Quality,
New Belgium Brewing Company

# ACKNOWLEDGMENTS

We would like to thank our industry colleagues whose continued input allowed for the significant updates included in this edition. We appreciate their expertise and commitment to consistently deliver the highest possible quality draught beer to the consumer. If we overlooked anyone who contributed, we sincerely apologize.

Special thanks are extended to Ken Grossman, President of Sierra Nevada Brewing Co. As the 2008 chair of the Brewers Association Technical Committee, Ken galvanized the creation of this manual through a collaborative effort with the brewing community, and we appreciate the time and dedication he and his colleagues put forth to bring this project to fruition.

**Contributors to the fourth edition**

**Jeff Bell,** MillerCoors a MolsonCoors Company
**Bridget Gaunter,** Bell's Brewery, Inc.
**Ernie Jimenez,** MillerCoors a MolsonCoors Company
**Charles Kyle,** Sierra Nevada Brewing Co.
**Matt Meadows,** New Belgium Brewing Company
**David Munro,** Bell's Brewery, Inc.
**Jeff Schaefer,** New Glarus Brewing Company (now of MillerCoors a Molson Coors Company)
**Ken Smith,** The Boston Beer Company
**Neil Witte,** Craft Quality Solutions
**Brewers Association Staff:** Damon Scott, Chuck Skypeck

**Contributors to previous editions**

Some of their past contributions remain part of the current version:

**Steve Armstrong,** MillerCoors a MolsonCoors Company
**Jeff Bell,** MillerCoors a MolsonCoors Company
**Todd Blondis,** MillerCoors a MolsonCoors Company
**Chris Bogdanoff,** Anaheim Brewery (now of Heroes Restaurant & Brewery)
**Ray Daniels,** Cicerone Certification Program
**Bridget Gaunter,** Bell's Brewery, Inc.
**Ben Geisthardt,** New Glarus Brewing Company
**Rob Gerrity,** Sierra Nevada Brewing Co. (now of Armadillo Insights)

Photo © Getty/Ridofranz

**Ken Grossman,** Sierra Nevada Brewing Co.
**Laura Harter,** Sierra Nevada Brewing Co.
**Cian Hickey,** Anheuser-Busch InBev (now of Micro Matic USA, Inc.)
**Ernie Jimenez,** MillerCoors a MolsonCoors Company
**Jaime Jurado,** Abita Brewing Company
(now of Ennoble Beverages)
**Charles Kyle,** Sierra Nevada Brewing Co.
**John Mallett,** Bell's Brewery, Inc.
**Matt Meadows,** New Belgium Brewing Company
**David Munro,** Bell's Brewery, Inc.
**Scott Nielsen,** MillerCoors a MolsonCoors Company
(now of Bedrock Training Solutions)
**Tim Raw,** Anheuser-Busch InBev (now of Barkau & Unverfehrt)
**Jeff Schaefer,** New Glarus Brewing Company
(now of MillerCoors a MolsonCoors Company)
**Martin Schuster,** Draught Beer Guild (now of Draught Beer Institute)
**Ken Smith,** The Boston Beer Company
**Matt Stinchfield,** Ploughshare Brewing Company
(now of Whalen Insurance)
**Zac Triemert,** Lucky Bucket Brewing Co.
(now of Brickway Brewery & Distillery)
**Josh Van Zee,** New Belgium Brewing Company
**Neil Witte,** Boulevard Brewing Company
(now of Craft Quality Solutions)
**Brewers Association Staff:** Paul Gatza, Charlie Papazian,
Bob Pease, Damon Scott, Chuck Skypeck, Tim Sloan,
Chris Swersey

We are grateful to our industry equipment suppliers who graciously allowed the use of their graphics and equipment information in various versions of this manual:

3M Food Safety
Analox Sensor Technology
Atlas Copco Compressors, LLC
Automatic Bar Controls, Inc.
Banner Equipment Company
Legacy US, LLC
McDantim, Inc.
Micro Matic USA, Inc.
Perlick Corporation
RLBS Ltd.
South-Tek Systems, LLC
Thonhauser GmbH
UK Brewing Supplies, Ltd.
Xylem, Inc.

Special thanks to New Belgium Brewing Company, Fort Collins, Colorado and The Post Brewing Co., Boulder, Colorado for use of their facilities for photography.

The Brewers Association wishes to thank the United States Department of Agriculture (USDA) and the Colorado State Department of Agriculture for their support and funding of version one of this project. State funds for this project were matched with federal funds under the Federal-State Marketing Improvement Program of the Agricultural Marketing Service, USDA.

Fourth edition © Brewers Association, 2019. ■

# INTRODUCTION

Walk into nearly any establishment that serves beer these days and you are likely to find draught beer for sale. But these days you will also see fancy options like nitro beers, effervescent German *weissbier*, and lightly carbonated English-style cask ales. Glassware also varies from run-of-the-mill pints to shapely half-liters and diminutive snifters, with every possible shape and size in between.

We find draught taps so often that we assume it must be relatively simple to keep and serve beer this way. But behind the simple flick of a handle that sends beer streaming into our glass at the bar you will find systems that require precise design, exact operating conditions, and careful, regular maintenance to ensure the proper flow of high-quality beer.

In this guide, we consider the equipment and anatomy of draught systems, then look at their operation and maintenance. We include a brief discussion of temporary systems, such as hand pumps and jockey boxes, but the majority of our attention is given to the two types of system usually seen in permanent installations: direct-draw and long-draw.

While equipment and system layout drive the initial performance of a draught system, other factors are equally important to the consumer's experience. To help you understand and operate your draught system, we look at the balancing equations that can keep perfect beer flowing from the taps. We also review pouring and glassware cleaning and show you how to check to see if a glass is "beer clean." Finally, we focus on the cleaning and maintenance of your draught system. Without regular and proper maintenance, your investment in draught technology won't bring you the dividends you expect. We conclude this manual by telling you what to look for when evaluating proper system maintenance, whether doing it yourself or supervising the work of a supplier.

To present this information, we have divided this manual into two sections. Section I focuses on draught system components and complete system layouts. From a simple hand-pump system at a party to a complex long-draw draught system, we review all the options.

Section II of this manual covers all the operation and maintenance issues for draught systems. It begins with a look at the details of pouring, glass cleaning, and other essentials of the perfect pint, before finishing with cleaning, maintenance, and troubleshooting. ■

# Section I

# DRAUGHT EQUIPMENT AND SYSTEM CONFIGURATIONS

Among draught systems, we find three general types based on equipment and design: temporary systems, direct-draw systems, and long-draw systems. In the course of this manual, we look closely at the layout, operation, and maintenance for each system. In Section I of this manual, we present four chapters that focus on system components, from faucets to tubing connectors, and explore how they are assembled to create different systems. Along the way we review important features of each component that can help prevent operating problems or beer quality issues in your system.

Before we jump into the components themselves, let's review some key concepts by looking briefly at the three sub-systems for draught: gas, beer, and cooling.

## GAS

Draught systems use carbon dioxide ($CO_2$) alone or mixed with nitrogen ($N_2$) in varying proportions depending on the requirements of the system and the beers being served. When properly selected and set, dispensing gas maintains the correct carbonation in the beer and helps to preserve its flavor. In most draught systems, the dispensing gas also propels beer from the keg to the faucet. Because the dispensing gas comes into direct contact with the beer, it must meet strict criteria for purity. Because of the damage it does, *compressed air should never be used to dispense draught beer*. For the purposes of this manual, as a convention in discussions involving mixed gas the proportion of $CO_2$ will always be shown first, followed by the proportion of $N_2$.

### BEER

Most draught systems use the gases mentioned above to drive beer from the keg through tubing to the faucet, where it will flow into the customer's glass. During the journey from keg to glass, beer should be protected from anything that would compromise its flavor or alter the carbonation level established by the brewery. The beer should flow through well-maintained beer lines manufactured from appropriate materials, and avoid any contact with brass parts that would impart a metallic flavor. Draught beer should flow at a specific rate and exit the faucet at the ideal carbonation level. The key to getting this right is balance between the applied gas pressure and the resistance provided by the tubing and fixtures the beer passes through during its journey to the bar.

### COOLING

The cooling system should hold beer at a constant temperature from keg to glass. Any increase in beer temperature between the cooler and the faucet can lead to dispensing problems such as foaming. In a simple direct-draw system, a refrigerated cabinet maintains the temperature of the keg and provides cooling to the beer as it travels the short distance to the faucet. Many long-draw systems use a walk-in cooler to cool the kegs, plus a system of tubes that circulate chilled glycol alongside the beer lines all the way to the faucet to ensure that the beer stays close to the temperature in the cooler all the way to the glass.

### ABOUT THIS SECTION

For each draught system, suitable equipment and designs must be chosen for each of these three components—gas, beer, and cooling. Section I of this manual details the equipment used in draught systems and the various system designs commonly employed.

**Chapter 1** examines nine components common to nearly all draught systems, including couplers, faucets, and beer lines. Understanding these basic elements will help you operate the draught systems you encounter. Of course, additional components are needed in more sophisticated systems—we introduce and discuss those, as well as look at the dynamics of carbonation, pressure, and system resistance, as we encounter them in **chapters 3 and 4**. By understanding these concepts and their relationship with each other, you'll be much better equipped for successful draught system operation. Once we have reviewed the common draught components, we will be ready to see how they get used in various system designs.

The simplest draught systems serve a temporary need. We find these systems at picnics, beer festivals, and other short-term events. In **chapter 2**, we cover the design, setup, use, and maintenance of the two main temporary systems: hand pumps and jockey boxes.

Moving to permanent draught installations, direct-draw systems offer the simplest approach. In **chapter 3**, we talk about the anatomy of a keg box, or "kegerator," and discuss how this basic approach is implemented in a walk-in cooler design. Both here and in **chapter 4**, we find some new components beyond the nine basic elements from the first chapter. In each chapter, we learn about the new components before looking at the anatomy of the overall system.

Permanent installations where the kegs cannot be located near the serving bar require long-draw systems. **Chapter 4** delves into the anatomy and operation of air-cooled and glycol-cooled long-draw systems, and also looks at beer pumps and mixed gas dispensing solutions for moving beer through long-draw systems. ■

### DRAUGHT BEER DISPENSING SYSTEMS

1

# ESSENTIAL DRAUGHT SYSTEM COMPONENTS

As a prelude to studying different draught system designs, let's review the equipment commonly found in all draught dispensing setups, from the backyard hand pump to the ballpark beer vendor. Here we cover nine components:

- Refrigeration/Cooling
- Kegs
- Couplers
- Tail Pieces and Connectors
- Beer Lines
- Faucets
- Gas Source
- Gas Lines
- Regulators

## REFRIGERATION/COOLING

Dispensing beer in a consistent and controlled manner requires that the beer traveling from keg to glass be maintained between 34°F and 38°F. While temporary systems may employ ice for cooling, most permanent installations employ refrigeration systems.

Cold box refrigeration systems can provide cooling for a small **direct-draw** box cooler or a large walk-in. The refrigeration itself can either be self-contained, with the compressor and condenser mounted on the unit, or use a remotely mounted compressor and condenser. Remotely mounting the compressor can benefit the installation by removing the source of heat from inside a room or building;

**Figure 1.1.** Common kegs sizes and their respective capacities and weights when full

| Capacity | ⅙ Barrel or cylinder | Pony keg (¼ barrel) | ¼ Barrel | Full-size keg (½ barrel) | Euro keg |
|---|---|---|---|---|---|
| Gallons | 5.16 | 7.75 | 7.75 | 15.5 | 13.2 |
| Fluid ounces | 660 | 992 | 992 | 1984 | 1690 |
| # of 12 oz. beers | 55 | 82 | 82 | 165 | 140 |
| Weight lb.(full) | 58 | 87 | 87 | 161 | 137 |

however, this requires additional refrigerant piping and possibly higher installation costs.

Condenser cooling can utilize either air or water; both methods have their strengths and weaknesses. In warm climates, air-cooled compressors can lose significant cooling capacity on a hot day when it is needed most. Water-cooled systems operate more efficiently, but require more maintenance and investment. Proper preventive care for either system is imperative (such as regularly cleaning condenser fins for air-cooled systems or cooling-water treatment for water-cooled systems) to prevent condenser fouling, which diminishes cooling capacity. Acid cleaning or **rodding** out the heat exchanger may be required to remedy condenser fouling. Many draught system problems are revealed on the first hot day of the season due to a lack of preventive maintenance. Although R22 refrigerant is still used in glycol systems, most new installations will utilize a more environmentally friendly substitute, such as R404a.

## KEGS

Kegs enable beer to be transported in bulk and dispensed by the glass while maintaining its quality and integrity. Keg design protects beer from both air and light while enabling it to be easily and rapidly dispensed. Keg sizes vary from approximately 5 to 15.5 gallons (fig. 1.1). Most brewers use kegs made of stainless steel, but you also see rubber-coated, aluminum, steel, and single-use kegs manufactured from various materials and utilizing differing technologies.

When tapped, the keg's valve admits gas to the head space, where it applies the pressure needed to push beer up through the **spear** or **downtube** and out of the keg through the coupler, while maintaining correct carbonation in the remaining beer.

Search for "keg guidelines" at https://www.BrewersAssociation.org for a complete discussion on performance of both refillable and single-use beer kegs.

### DRAUGHT SAFETY

Kegs are pressurized vessels and can be dangerous if mishandled. The lock ring of a drop-in valve should never be removed in the field. A threaded valve can be inadvertently loosened or become unseated when disengaging a coupler, creating a potentially dangerous situation. Keg valves should never be removed in the field. Kegs should only be serviced by trained personnel.

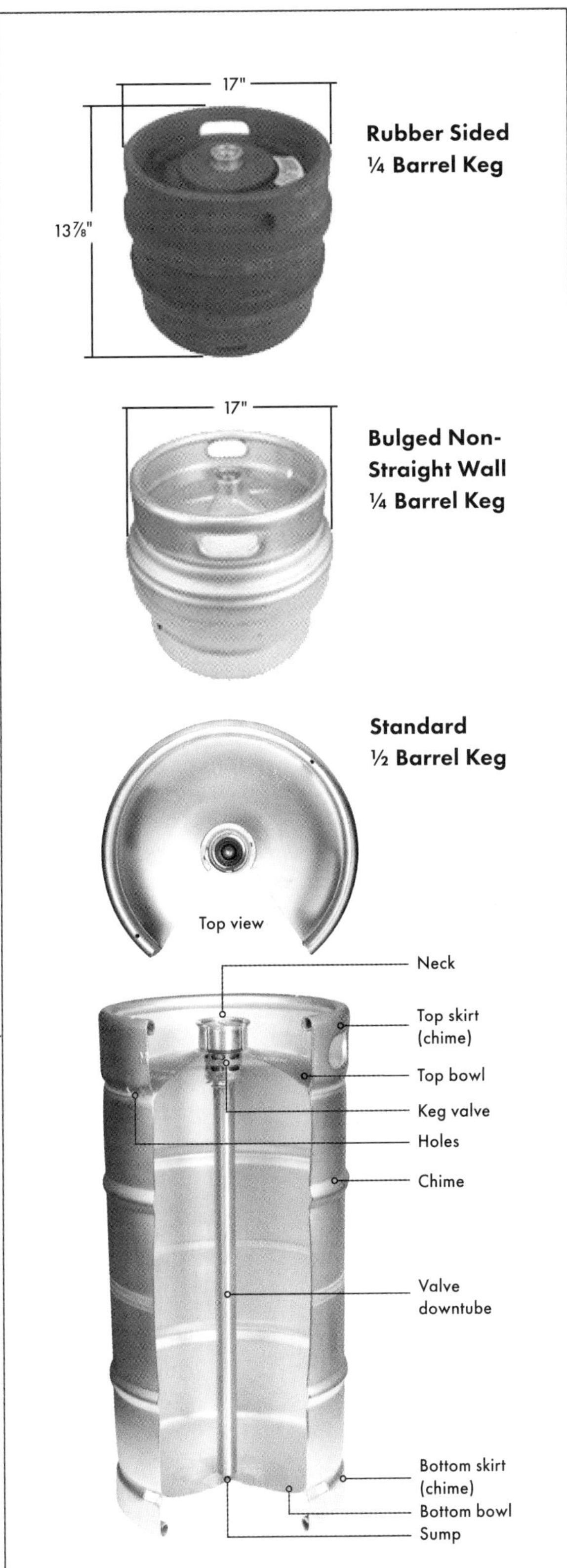


**Figure 1.2.** Examples of common keg types, showing a rubber-coated ¼ barrel keg *(top)*, a bulged non-straight wall ¼ barrel keg *(middle)*, and a standard ½ barrel keg. The ½ barrel keg is shown in cutaway view with major features labeled.

## KEG VALVES

Kegs are pressurized vessels and can be dangerous if mishandled. Nearly all modern kegs use some form of **Sankey** valve and stem. There are two main types of Sankey valves and corresponding keg necks: drop-in and threaded. From a user standpoint, the valves function identically; from above, the valves appear nearly indistinguishable to the untrained eye. Drop-in Sankey valves are held in place by a lock ring or circlip. ***The lock ring and valve should never be removed in the field*** because pressure in the keg can cause the valve and downtube to move upward with high velocity. Very rarely, a lock ring can fail, possibly loosening the valve, creating a potentially dangerous situation. Threaded Sankey valves screw into the neck of the keg. Very rarely, a threaded valve can be inadvertently loosened or become unseated when disengaging a coupler, creating a potentially dangerous situation. ***Keg valves should never be removed in the field.*** Kegs should only be serviced by trained personnel. New O-rings and lock rings should always be installed when replacing a keg valve. All new parts should be supplied by, or approved by, the keg valve manufacturer.

Older keg designs that use different tapping methods are rarely encountered and are not covered here.

### SANKEY VALVES AND KEG NECKS

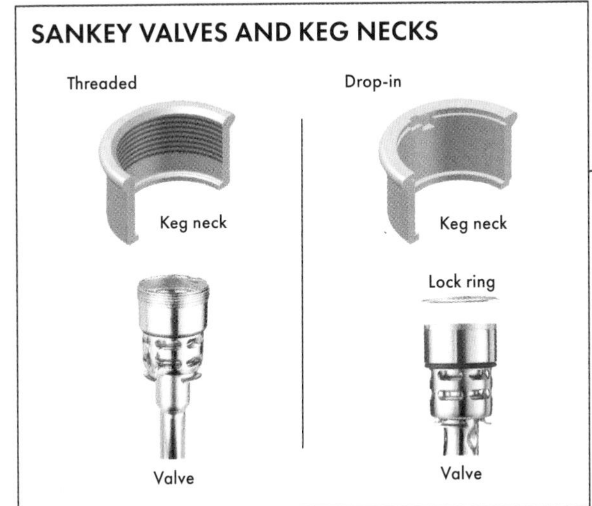


**Figure 1.3.** Sankey valves and keg necks.

## SINGLE-USE KEGS

A fast growing segment in keg technology is the single-use keg. Single-use kegs should not be reused, for beer or any other purpose. They should be depressurized and disposed of correctly after being emptied. There are many types of single-use kegs available on the market, and some require specialized filling and/or tapping couplers that may require specific training to use.

To prevent keg rupture, use a pressure regulator and properly sized relief device with the pressure source to which the keg is connected. Filling and dispensing systems should be set and checked regularly to maintain a pressure lower than the weakest component. Single-use kegs should never be cleaned using any keg cleaning equipment. The pressures, chemicals, and temperatures used for keg cleaning may compromise the structural integrity of a single-use keg.

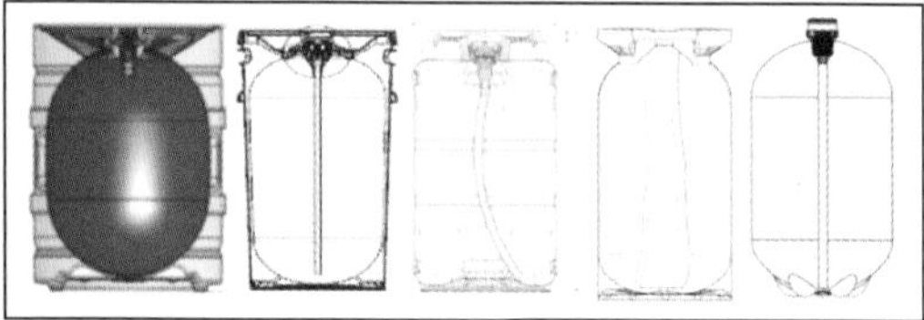

**Figure 1.4.** Examples of single-use keg configurations.

## COUPLERS

Gas flows in and beer flows out of a keg through the coupler. While this device has many casual names in beer cellars around the country, the industry adopted the term **coupler** as the standard term for the device.

When you attach a coupler to a keg, a probe depresses a ball, or poppet, in the keg valve, allowing carbon dioxide ($CO_2$) or mixed gas to enter the keg, thereby applying pressure to the beer. This forces the beer to travel up the spear, through the beer lines, and to the **faucet**.

The coupler is typically attached to a flexible vinyl beer line (referred to as a **jumper line**) using a washer, tail piece, and hex nut. In the United States, the threads on hex nuts and couplers are sized to the "Cleveland thread" standard, which is 29/32" diameter and 14 threads per inch pitch. Be aware that couplers from other countries may use differently sized threads. Check for leaks after installing a hex nut onto any coupler.

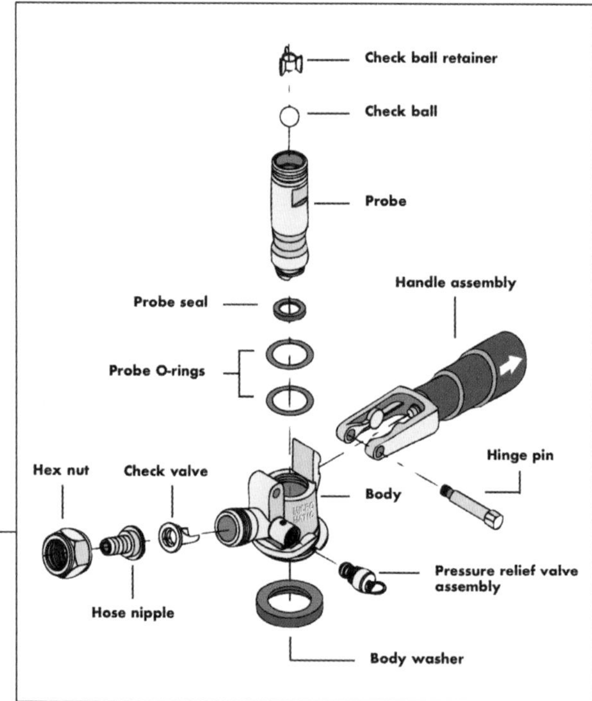


**Figure 1.5.** "D" system coupler with individual components shown.

Couplers include two types of one-way valve:

- A **check valve** allows $CO_2$ to flow into the keg but prevents the beer from backing up into the gas line if gas pressure drops, which protects the gas regulators from damage. (Check valves are removed when kegs are linked in series; see page 51.)

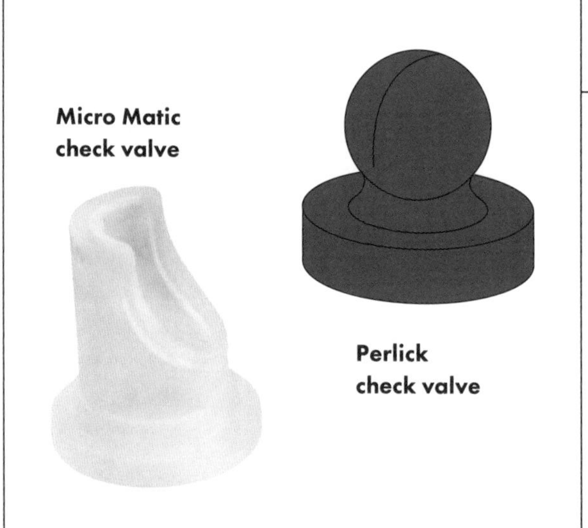


**Figure 1.6.** Common types of coupler one-way valves.

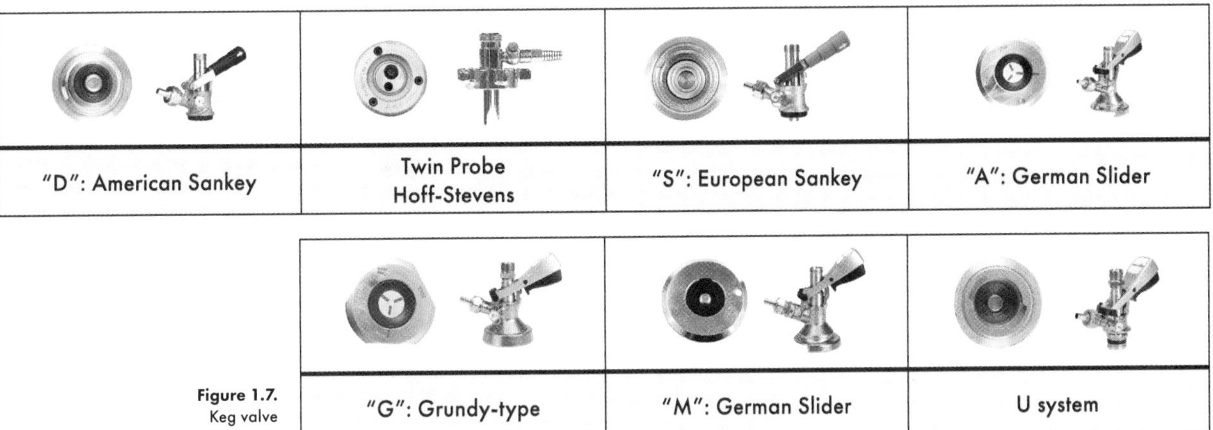


**Figure 1.7.** Keg valve systems.

- A **check ball** valve prevents beer from the beer line flowing out through the coupler when the coupler is disconnected from the keg. This prevents beer spillage in areas where kegs are tapped.

A keg coupler should also contain an integral pressure relief valve. If excessive gas pressure were applied to a keg, this valve should open to prevent injury and damage to the keg and coupler. The safety relief valve can also be opened manually, which should be done periodically for safety testing to check the relief valve works. The manual release usually looks like a small metal pin fitted with a wire ring (see example in fig. 1.8). To test the valve, pull on the ring to slide the pin a short distance out of the coupler and release a small amount of gas.

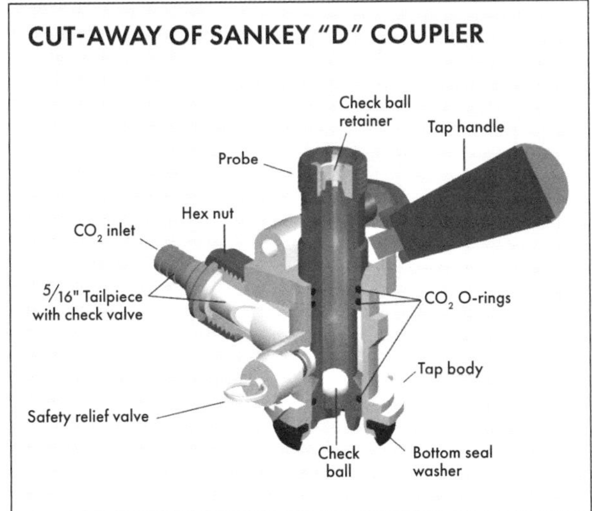


**Figure 1.8.** A cutaway of a Sankey "D" system coupler shows all the features of a typical coupler.

At the time of writing, most breweries worldwide use keg valves compatible with one of seven variations of the Sankey-type coupler (fig. 1.7). Most US breweries use the Sankey "D" coupler; use of "D" couplers will be assumed for the purposes of this manual unless noted otherwise. A few US breweries still use the twin probe Hoff-Stevens valve and coupler system.

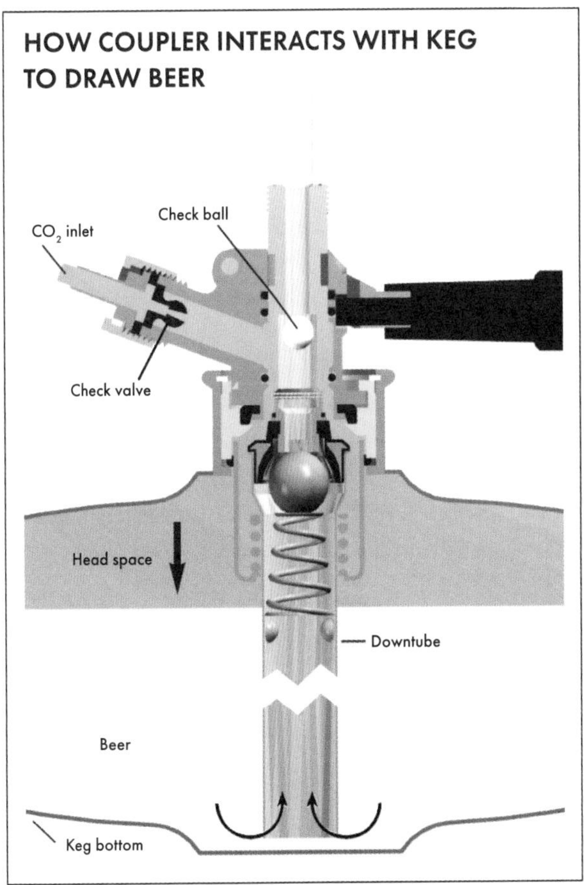


**Figure 1.9.** How a coupler interacts with a keg to draw beer.

### TAIL PIECES AND CONNECTORS

**Tail pieces** connect couplers, wall brackets, **shanks**—or any other piece of equipment—to vinyl tubing or other types of beer line. Tail pieces come in several sizes to match common tubing diameters. They are held in place with a hex nut and sealing washer. A clamp secures the tubing to the tail piece on the barbed side. A wing or hex nut and sealing washer attach the tail piece to the coupler or other equipment on its flat side. In the United States, hex nut and coupler threads are the "Cleveland thread" standard size, which is 29/32" diameter with 14 threads per inch pitch.

**Figure 1.10.** Tail piece and parts to attach it.

## METAL PARTS AND HYGIENIC DESIGN

For many years, suppliers made metal parts for draught systems with chrome-plated brass. While chrome has no negative effect on beer quality, beer that has any contact with brass reacts and picks up a metallic off-taste. Exposed brass is also difficult to clean. While the coating on chrome-plated parts rarely wears away on the outside, cleaning and beer flow eventually expose the brass on the inside, bringing the beer into contact with the brass.

To avoid brass contact, brewers recommend stainless steel parts for draught dispensing. In addition to being inert in contact with beer, stainless steel parts are easier to clean and help maintain high-quality draught dispensing.

Manufacturers offer all faucets, shanks, tail pieces, splicers, wall brackets, and probes mentioned in this manual in stainless steel. If your system already contains chrome-plated brass components, inspect the beer contact surfaces regularly and replace those components as soon as any brass is exposed.

All system components should be designed to facilitate cleaning and to preclude contamination, particularly microbial growth. Indentations, recesses, dead space, and gaps should be avoided. Edges at protrusions, transitions, and extensions should be rounded. Chosen components should be designed so they permit an unobstructed flow of liquids and are easy to drain.

### BEER LINE

Between coupler and faucet, beer travels through **beer line** selected to fit the needs of the specific draught application. Options range from vinyl to specialized **barrier tubing** and even stainless steel.

Most draught systems use clear vinyl tubing for all or part of the beer line. In hand pump and direct-draw systems, beer often runs most of or the entire route from coupler to faucet in vinyl tubing. In long-draw systems, beer commonly passes through two different sections of vinyl hose but travels most of the way through special barrier tubing that prevent the ingress of oxygen and other gases (see chapter 4). Vinyl tubing is highly flexible and is best used where lines are not secured in place and where it can easily be replaced. Vinyl tubing should be replaced every one to two years, because it is relatively porous and susceptible to bacterial and flavor contamination.

It should also be noted that new types of beer line with new technologies are entering the market. One such beer line does have barrier properties but is made of polymers that keep the line flexible and are mostly vinyl free. It is not recommended that this next generation of beer line be used to replace current barrier tubing in long-draw systems, but it would be preferable as a replacement where vinyl is currently being used.

We will discuss other types of tubing later on as the topics for their use present themselves. These other types of tubing include:

- colored vinyl and braided vinyl used for $CO_2$ gas;
- stainless steel tubing found in **jockey boxes** and tap towers;
- barrier tubing, which is a low-resistance, easy-to-clean beer line for long-draw systems;
- **polyethylene** tubing used to carry glycol coolant.

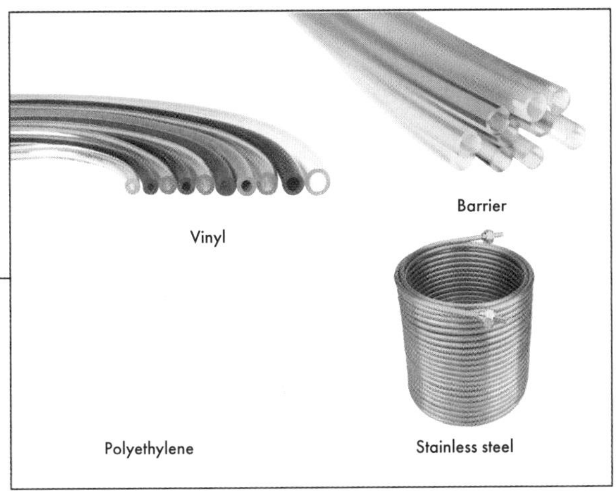


**Figure 1.11.** Examples of tubing used in beer line.

## FAUCETS

Faucets dispense beer to the glass. They often hold the tap marker to identify the type of beer being dispensed. The most common faucets are generally suitable for dispensing both ales and lagers. The most common faucet in the United States is rear-sealing and has vent holes that need to be carefully cleaned and inspected during routine cleanings. The vents provide back pressure that allows for smooth beer flow and permits the faucet to drain between pours. Ventless, or forward-sealing, faucets are easy to clean and are available in stainless steel. Several other designs are widely available and are used either for their aesthetic appeal or for serving a specific style of beer (table 1.1, figs. 1.12, 1.14). Nitrogen, or nitro, faucets are used for nitrogenized beers, such as certain stouts. These faucets use a diaphragm to stop beer flow when the handle is in the off position. A restrictor plate forces the beer through tiny holes to facilitate the breakout of nitrogen within the faucet nozzle. Nitro faucets, like all faucets, need to be completely disassembled and cleaned as part of every line cleaning regimen. Nitrogenized beer is covered in more detail in chapter 4, page 42.

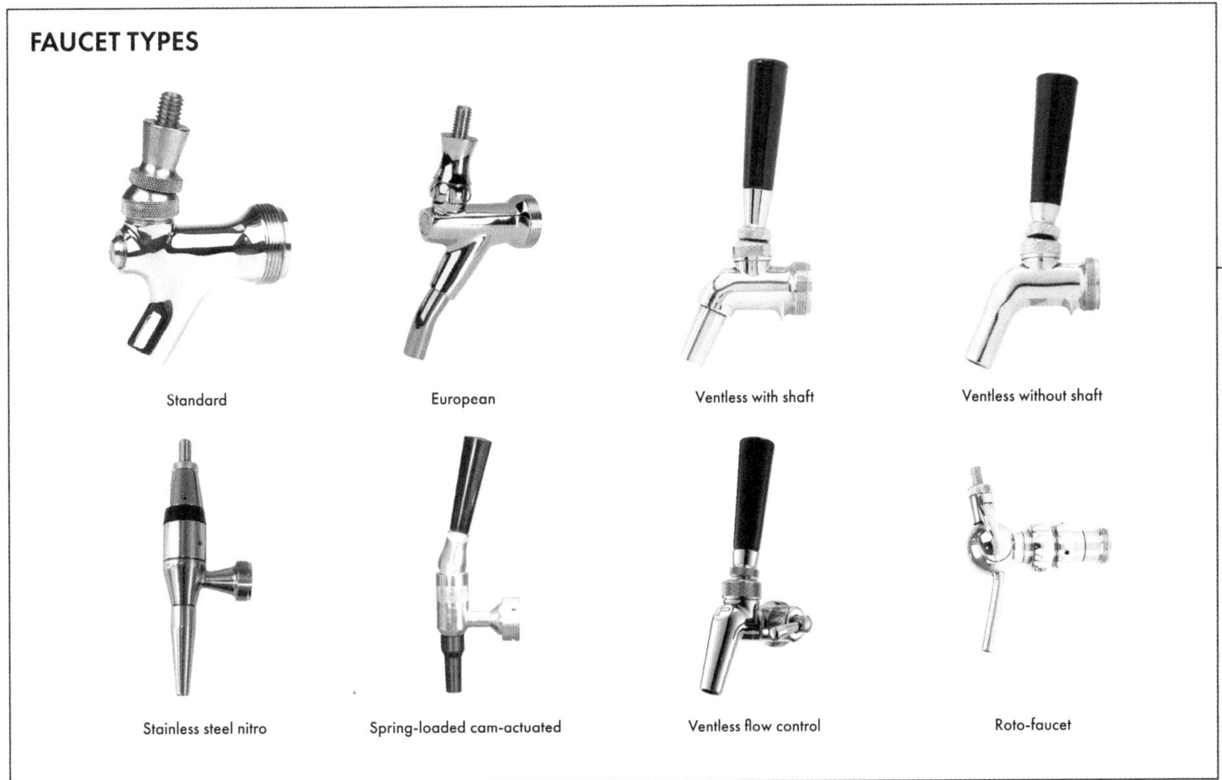


**Figure 1.12.** Faucet designs commonly used to dispense ales and lagers. The pros and cons of each design are listed in table 1.1.

At retail, most faucets are fitted with tap markers that clearly display the brand being dispensed; in many states this is required. The tap marker must be aligned properly in order to be read easily by the consumer and sales staff. The tap marker is fitted with a standard-sized threaded sleeve for easy installation onto the faucet lever; in many cases, however, the tap marker may not be aligned properly when seated fully on the lever. For this reason, nearly all faucets are also fitted with a lever collar or handle jacket on the lever. These allow the tap marker to be aligned properly, as well as installed securely. When installing the tap marker on the faucet lever, check to make sure it's aligned appropriately. If not, unscrew the marker just enough to align it correctly, then back the lever collar up under the marker, and tighten the tap marker snugly onto the lever collar or handle jacket (fig. 1.13).

In the United States, all faucets attach to shanks with a standard thread size of 1⅛" diameter and 18 threads per inch pitch. Be aware that faucets from other countries may use different thread sizes and may require adapters or special shanks.

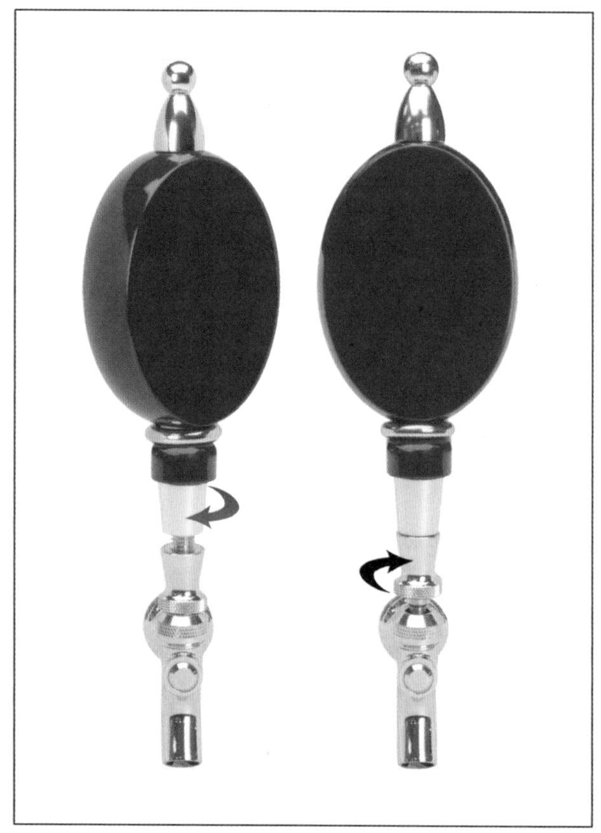

**Figure 1.13. Securing tap marker to faucet.**

**TABLE 1.1.** PROS AND CONS OF VARIOUS FAUCET DESIGNS

| Type | Valve | Flow | Pro | Con |
|---|---|---|---|---|
| **Standard** | Vertical, seals in back of shaft | Smooth | Low velocity | Barrel interior susceptible to microbial growth |
| **European** | Vertical, seals in back of shaft | Smooth | Low velocity | Barrel interior susceptible to microbial growth; may have threads that differ from standard US thread size |
| **Ventless with shaft** | Vertical, seals in front of shaft | Slightly twisting | Low susceptibility to microbial growth | High velocity flow may result in turbulence |
| **Ventless without shaft** | Vertical, seals in front of faucet body | Slightly twisting | Low susceptibility to microbial growth | High velocity flow may result in turbulence |
| **Nitro** | Spring-loaded cam-actuated plunger-style valve. Restrictor plate and flow straightener in nozzle | Cascade of tiny bubbles | Gives unique texture needed for nitro beers | Nozzle susceptible to microbial growth from beer retained inside narrow opening; small nozzle parts require manual cleaning; use only with nitro beers |
| **Spring-loaded cam-actuated** | Horizontal, top of nozzle | Slightly twisting | Low susceptibility to microbial growth | Nozzle susceptible to microbial growth from beer retained inside narrow opening; many small parts to clean |
| **Ventless flow control** | Vertical, seals in back of shaft | Smooth, adjustable flow rate | Adjustable velocity may allow for increased dispensing pressure | Nozzle interior susceptible to microbial growth |
| **Roto-faucet** | Internal, rotating ball | Rapid velocity | Few parts, simple to clean | Some flow turbulence |

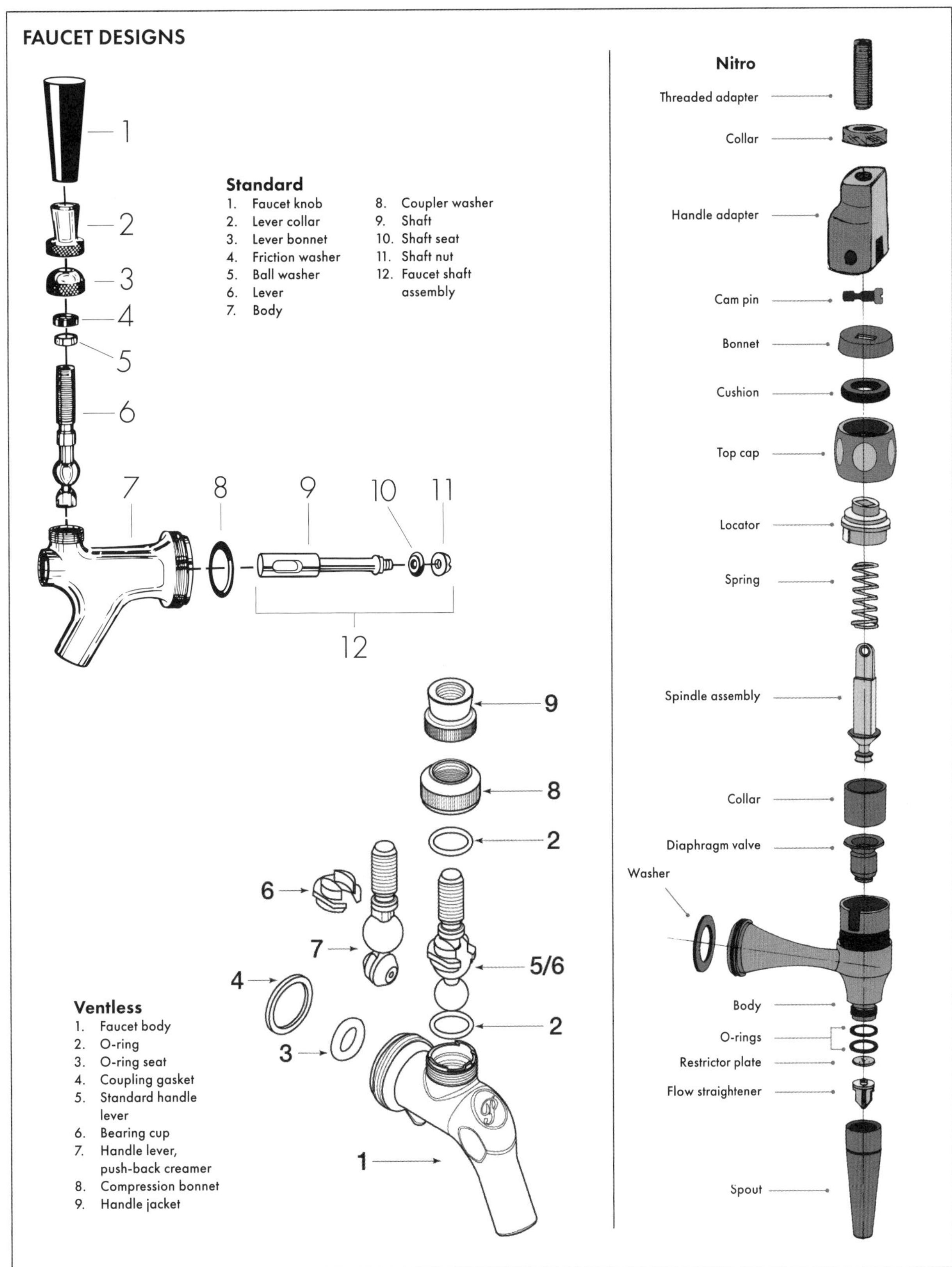


**Figure 1.13.** Exploded view of three different faucet designs: standard, ventless, and nitro.

## SHANKS

Most draught systems firmly mount the faucet to either a **tower** or a wall, making it a stable point for dispensing beer. A threaded shank with securing nuts creates a solid connection to the supporting tower or wall. The faucet then connects to one side of the shank and the beer line connects to the other side by either an attached nipple or a tail piece connected with the usual washer and nut. Today, shanks with ¼" bore diameters are most commonly available and recommended in the United States. Shanks with a 3⁄16" bore diameter are also available, but they are less common. The once-common practice of drilling out 3⁄16" bore shanks to a larger diameter is not recommended. This practice was only practical on chrome-plated or all-brass shanks and resulted in exposed brass, which compromises beer quality. Inappropriately sized shanks (and brass shanks in general) should be replaced with correctly sized stainless steel shanks.

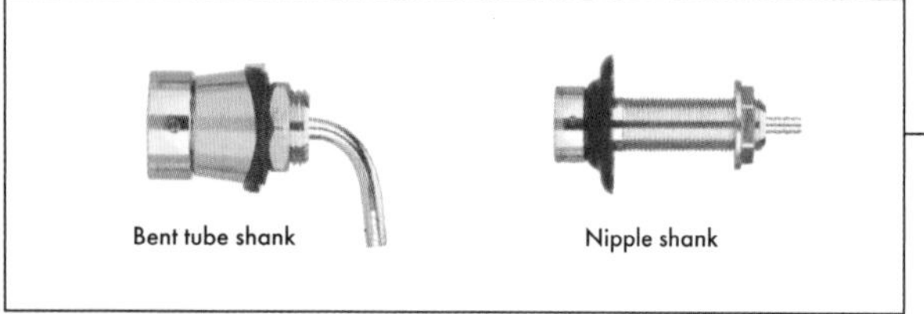


**Figure 1.15.** Common shank types.

**Figure 1.16.** Bent tube shank installed in a single-tower kegerator.

Photo © Aaron Colussi (mounted shank)

## GAS SOURCE

Draught systems depend on gas pressure to push beer from the keg to the faucet. To achieve this, kegs should be pressurized with $CO_2$, or a $CO_2$ and nitrogen (**$N_2$**) mix. Consult chapter 4 to determine the proper blend of $CO_2$ and $N_2$ for individual applications.

### DRAUGHT SAFETY

When transporting compressed gas cylinders, the valve should be turned off with the regulator removed. Proper transportation should be in a manner that prevents cylinders from creating a hazard by tipping, falling, or rolling. Do not attempt to lift a cylinder by its valve.

Gas used for dispensing beer should be "beverage grade." Gas selection and purity affect the freshness and quality of the beer served through the draught system. Remember, the gas you use fills the keg as the beer drains. Thus, off-flavors or impurities in the gas quickly migrate to the beer and spoil its freshness and flavor. Compressed air should never be used to pressurize a keg because the oxygen in the air generates stale flavors in beer within just a few hours. All gas used for dispensing beer should meet the specifications of the International Society of Beverage Technologists or the Compressed Gas Association (*see* appendix A).

### NO AIR COMPRESSORS, PLEASE!

Systems that use compressed air as a dispensing gas expose beer to oxygen, which produces paper- or cardboard-like aromas and flavors in the beer. Brewers go to great lengths to keep oxygen out of beer to avoid these undesirable stale characteristics. Air compressors also push contaminants from the outside atmosphere into the keg, increasing the chance of bacterial spoilage and off-flavors. For these reasons, compressed air should never be used in direct contact with beer.

Retailers may purchase beverage grade gas in cylinders that will be delivered by the gas vendor and swapped out when empty. Such cylinders are filled, maintained, and inspected by the vendor. High-volume users may purchase a bulk gas vessel known as a **dewar** that will be filled on location from a bulk gas truck. Bulk tanks can provide $CO_2$ for both soda and beer.

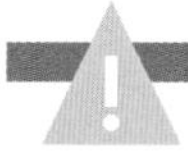

## DRAUGHT SAFETY

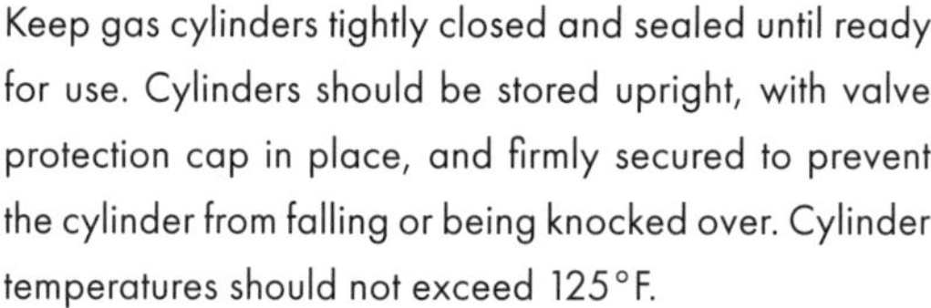

Keep gas cylinders tightly closed and sealed until ready for use. Cylinders should be stored upright, with valve protection cap in place, and firmly secured to prevent the cylinder from falling or being knocked over. Cylinder temperatures should not exceed 125°F.

$CO_2$ tanks contain both liquid and gas phases. The tank pressure is dependent on ambient temperature and, regardless of tank fill level, will vary from 600 to 1200 **psi** until empty. For safety reasons, $CO_2$ tanks should never be located inside the refrigerator or **walk-in cooler** because a leak can fill the space with deadly $CO_2$. Refrigerated storage also decreases gas yield compared with $CO_2$ stored at ambient temperatures.

## DRAUGHT SAFETY

***Breathing high concentrations of $CO_2$ can be deadly!*** Take care to prevent $CO_2$ buildup in enclosed spaces such as cold boxes. System leaks or beer pumps using $CO_2$ can cause this gas to accumulate in the cooler. To prevent this, beer pumps driven by $CO_2$ must be vented to the atmosphere. $CO_2$ warning alarms are available and recommended for installations with enclosed areas, such as walk-in coolers that contain $CO_2$ fittings and gas lines.

### Gas Filters

Beverage grade $CO_2$ comes from many commercial and industrial operations and is supplied for many uses besides beverages (e.g., fire extinguishers, welding, food processing, etc.). $CO_2$ bottles can be contaminated by poor handling and storage. They can be contaminated by beer or soft drinks if a check valve malfunctions and the beer or soft drink flows back into an empty $CO_2$ bottle. Installing a gas filter helps reduce the likelihood that any contaminants in the gas reach the beer. Filters must be replaced periodically per the manufacturer's instructions. Be sure to follow manufacturer recommendations for filter maintenance.

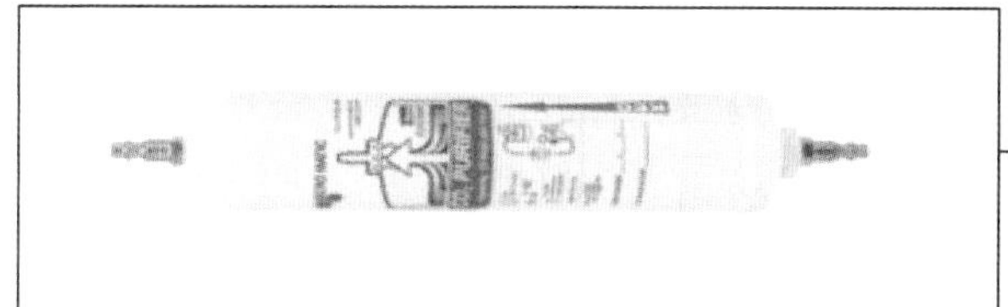

**Figure 1.17.** In-line gas filter.

### Gas Leak Detectors

Gas leaks in a draught system not only cost money in lost gas, but may also cause pressure drops that can lead to foamy beer. In enclosed spaces large $CO_2$ leaks can be extremely dangerous and even deadly. Gas leak detectors are available that are plumbed directly into the gas supply line to the draught system. When no beer is being poured, a float inside the device will rise if gas is leaking.

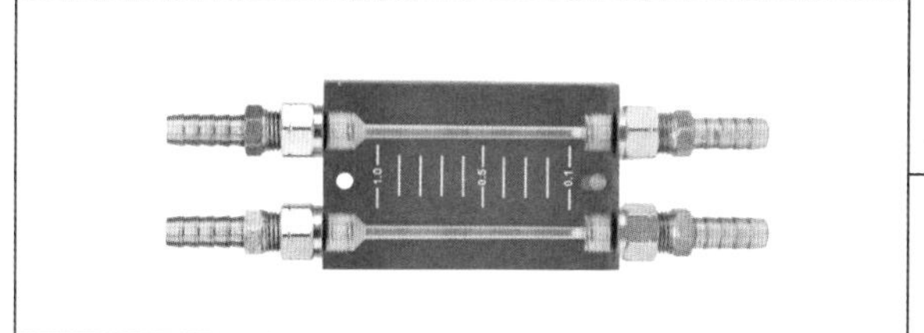

**Figure 1.18.** In-line gas leak detector.

## GAS LINE

**Gas line** should be selected to withstand the pressures in the draught system. Vinyl tubing intended to be used as gas line often has a greater wall thickness than vinyl beer line tubing. To help distinguish between gas line and beer line, colored vinyl is usually used for $CO_2$ supply line. Colored vinyl should not be used for beer because it prevents visual inspection. An exception to this rule would be line exposed to sunlight, for example, at an outdoor festival using a jockey box. Clear vinyl, or translucent colored vinyl, may also be used for the gas line as it aids in troubleshooting by allowing you to see if beer has escaped the coupler and entered the gas line due to a faulty or missing check valve. Because vinyl gas line will fail at high pressures, it can also serve as an important safety feature in the event of secondary regulator failure by rupturing before a keg becomes over-pressurized.

Braided vinyl is often used for $CO_2$, particularly in high-pressure situations (50+ psi) and in long $CO_2$ runs. Braided vinyl is commonly used in soft drink lines for both beverage and gas.

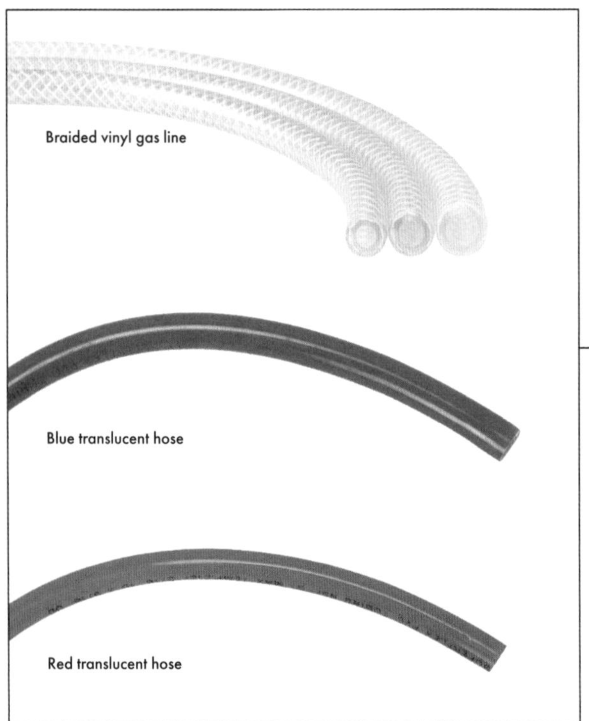


**Figure 1.19.** Examples of tubing used for gas lines. Red translucent hose is used for $CO_2$ and blue translucent hoses run $N_2$. However, best practice is to use translucent line so any growth can be seen with visual inspection of the gas line.

## REGULATORS

A regulator adjusts and controls the flow of gas from any source. Each regulator typically has at least one, and often two, pressure gauges that help in setting the outlet pressure and monitoring the gas level in the tank. Valves and an adjustment screw control the actual flow of gas from source to destination.

All gas systems employ a primary regulator attached to the gas source, namely a portable bottle or bulk tank. The primary regulator typically contains two gauges: one high-pressure gauge showing the tank or supply pressure, and a second low-pressure gauge showing what is being delivered to the keg. Some simpler regulators may contain only one gauge displaying the delivered pressure, making it more difficult to predict when the bottle is getting low. Some suppliers provide jockey box regulators preset with no gauges, since the gauges are easily damaged in transit.

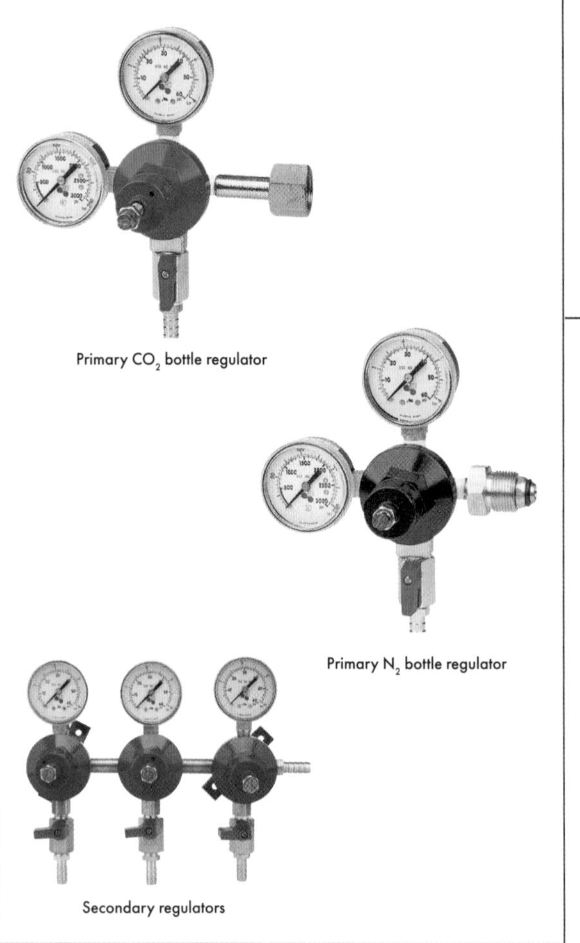


**Figure 1.20.** Common types of gas flow regulator.

Primary regulators are attached to the gas bottle with either an integrated O-ring seal in the face of the regulator fitting, or a fiber or Teflon flat washer. These parts need to be replaced occasionally to prevent leaks and should be inspected every time the bottle is changed. Many primary regulators are also equipped with one or more shut-off valves located on the low-pressure outlet, allowing the $CO_2$ to be shut off without changing the set-screw or shutting off the main tank valve.

A primary regulator must also contain a safety relief valve to prevent dangerous system pressures in case of a malfunction or frozen regulator. Bottled $CO_2$ pressure can exceed 1000 psi, creating an extreme hazard if not handled properly.

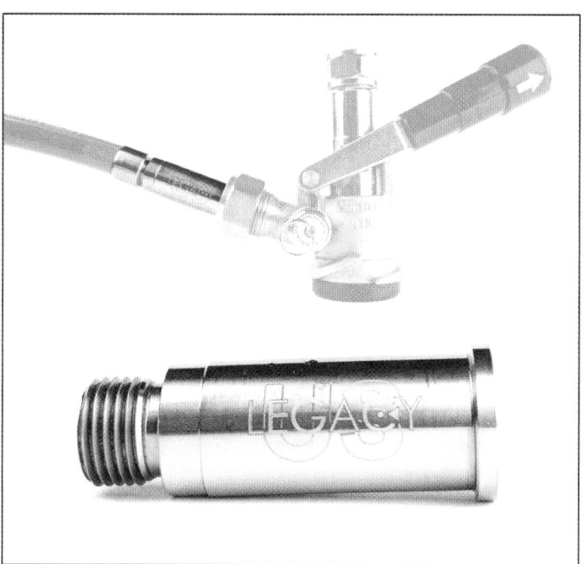


**Figure 1.21.** The Gov Reg™ replaces traditional secondary pressure regulators and installs on a keg coupler, gas manifold, or inline. A proprietary tool is used to set the pressure, which prevents tampering and unwanted pressure adjustments.

The pressure to each keg is typically governed by a separate regulator, known as a secondary regulator. Chapter 4 has more information on how to set secondary regulators properly, but it should be noted that a primary regulator that feeds several secondary regulators needs to be set about 5–10 psi above the highest setting of the secondary regulators. If the primary regulator were set at the same number as the secondaries, then only one faucet could be open at a time since the pressure from the source would be only enough to support one line at a time.

Gaugeless regulators have a fixed pressure, connect directly to the coupler, and can only be adjusted with a proprietary tool. The gas line must be rated to withstand the pressure supplied from the gas source.

Nitrogen regulators are designed for higher pressures and have a male thread with a conical fitting that (depending on the design) seats to the gas source with or without an O-ring.

### PRESSURE AND PRESSURE GAUGES

For the purposes of this manual, pressure is the amount of force acting on the surface of beer in a keg or serving vessel, and is often expressed in pounds per square inch (psi). **Absolute pressure** is the total pressure on the beer, and is the sum of atmospheric pressure plus any additional applied pressure from the dispensing gas. **Atmospheric pressure** is the amount of force exerted by the weight of air in the Earth's atmosphere above an object. At sea level, atmospheric pressure is equal to 14.7 psi. If the dispensing gas is applied at 15 psi, then the absolute pressure on the beer is 29.7 psi (14.7 psi + 15 psi).

Pressure can be measured several ways. Most pressure gauges are designed to measure the pressure of the dispensing gas applied to beer beyond the local atmospheric pressure level. This is called **gauge pressure**, usually given as pounds per square inch, gauge (**psig**). Gauges in draught beer systems will nearly always read in psig. (Some specialized gauges are designed to measure the total pressure on the beer, or absolute pressure, in units of **psia**; these are very rare in draught beer dispensing systems.)

As draught beer is dispensed, *the carbonation level will depend on the absolute pressure of the dispensing gas, not the gauge pressure of the dispensing gas.* This is true for both 100% $CO_2$ as well as blended gas. The carbonation level in a beer is set by the brewer to maximize flavor, aroma, and presentation. One goal of draught beer dispensing is to maintain carbonation level. If the absolute pressure of the dispensing gas is too high, the carbonation level of the beer will increase over time. If the absolute pressure of the dispensing gas is too low, the carbonation level of the beer will decrease over time. More information about this very important topic can be found in appendix C.

### Elevation Affects Pressure

Because atmospheric pressure changes depending on elevation, therefore so does the absolute pressure. So you need to take elevation into account when designing draught beer dispensing systems and when you read carbonation tables. At higher elevations, the layer of air is thinner and therefore weighs less, so atmospheric pressure is also less. Atmospheric pressure decreases by about 1 psi per 2000 feet gained in elevation. To account for this loss of pressure, a good rule of thumb is to add 1 psi to the regulator setting for every 2000 feet gained in elevation.

Let's look at an example in which the ideal dispensing gas pressure for a beer brand in a particular draught beer system at sea level is determined to be 15 psig. At sea level, atmospheric pressure is equal to 14.7 psi, so at sea level a keg of beer with dispensing gas pressure of 15 psig is under an absolute pressure of 29.7 psia (15 psig + 14.7 psi). That same keg of beer at an altitude of 5000 feet with the same dispensing gas pressure of 15 psig is only under 27.2 psia (15 psig + 14.7 psi – 2.5 psi).

Table 1.2 illustrates the absolute pressure on a keg of beer at different elevations, assuming 15 psig dispensing gas pressure. Even though the pressure gauge on the keg of beer reads the same, the absolute pressure of the dispensing gas in the keg is decreasing with elevation. Over time, the carbonation level of the beer being dispensed at a higher elevation will slowly decrease because the absolute pressure of the dispensing gas is lower than at sea level.

Table 1.3 illustrates that the gauge pressure of the dispensing gas needs to be increased above the calculated dispense pressure at sea level in order to maintain the carbonation level of beer being dispensed at elevation. ■

**TABLE 1.2.** ABSOLUTE PRESSURE DECREASES AS ELEVATION INCREASES WHEN DISPENSING PRESSURE IS HELD AT THE SAME PSIG.

| **Elevation** (ft. above sea level) | **Atmospheric pressure** (psi) | **Dispensing pressure** (psig) | **Absolute pressure** (psia) |
|---|---|---|---|
| **0** | 14.7 | 15 | 29.7 |
| **2,000** | 13.7 | 15 | 28.7 |
| **4,000** | 12.7 | 15 | 27.7 |
| **5,000** | 12.2 | 15 | 27.2 |
| **8,000** | 10.7 | 15 | 25.7 |
| **10,000** | 9.7 | 15 | 24.7 |

**TABLE 1.3.** DISPENSING PRESSURE MUST BE INCREASED AS ELEVATION INCREASES TO MAINTAIN ABSOLUTE PRESSURE, PSIA.

| **Elevation** (ft. above sea level) | **Atmospheric pressure** (psi) | **Dispensing pressure** (psig) | **Absolute pressure** (psia) |
|---|---|---|---|
| **0** | 14.7 | 15 | 29.7 |
| **2,000** | 13.7 | 16 | 29.7 |
| **4,000** | 12.7 | 17 | 29.7 |
| **5,000** | 12.2 | 17.5 | 29.7 |
| **8,000** | 10.7 | 19 | 29.7 |
| **10,000** | 9.7 | 20 | 29.7 |

2

# TEMPORARY DRAUGHT DISPENSING SYSTEMS

Draught beer goes great with outdoor events, but the temporary setting prohibits use of traditional direct-draw or long-draw draught equipment. Instead, we usually use one of two different systems, hand pumps or jockey boxes.

## HAND PUMPS

Hand pumps allow draught beer to be dispensed for a one-day occasion or event. These systems compromise accepted standards of draught dispensing in order to offer a simple method for serving draught beer.

In the simplest systems, the beer flows to a simple faucet attached to a short section of vinyl hose (fig. 2.1 *left* and *middle*). Gas pressure comes from compressed air introduced by way of a hand-operated pump integrated into the coupler.

Since these simple systems introduce compressed air into the keg, they are suitable only for situations where the beer will be consumed in a single day. Also, these dispensing systems typically do not produce the best serving results, since balancing the correct top pressure is very imprecise. For best results, the keg must be kept in ice and consistently—but not excessively—pumped as the contents are dispensed. Pumping the keg with the faucet closed will only serve to build up pressure in the head space, encouraging the absorption of oxygen into the beer.

Improved designs use single-use $CO_2$ cartridges with an integrated regulator (fig. 2.1 *right*). These units may also include a traditional vented faucet mounted on a short length of stainless steel beer line. This design overcomes the key shortcomings of hand-pumped taps.

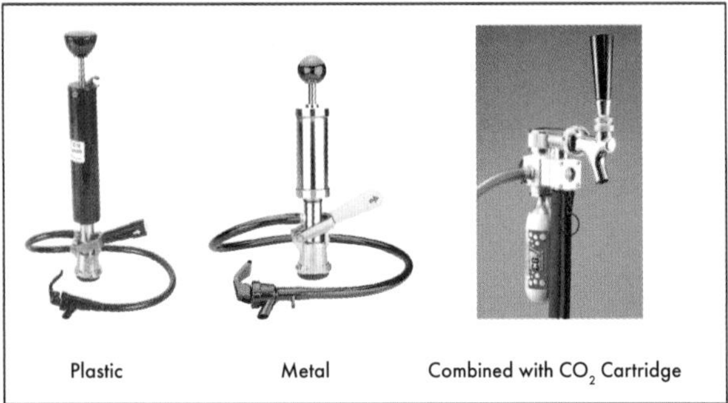


**Figure 2.1.** Common temporary beer dispensing equipment, showing a simple plastic *(left)* and metal *(middle)* hand pump, and a hand pump combined with a $CO_2$ cartridge with integrated regulator *(right)*.

## JOCKEY BOXES

Jockey boxes offer a superior temporary dispensing system. In a jockey box system, a normal coupler is attached to the keg and $CO_2$ is used to pressurize the system. Beer passes through a **cold plate** or stainless steel **coil** that is submerged in ice (fig. 2.2). The beer is **flash chilled** to the proper dispensing temperature. A jockey box equipped with a cold plate uses ice to cool beer flowing through the cold plate (ice water should be avoided as it is too cold and could freeze residual water or low-alcohol beer in the internal lines of the plate). A jockey box equipped with stainless steel coil uses ice and water to chill beer flowing through the coil.

Jockey boxes are not appropriate for day-to-day use, as draught beer is perishable and room temperature storage accelerates aging. The high-pressure $CO_2$ used can also overcarbonate a typical keg when tapped longer than a day. Partial kegs remaining from temporary service are not usable in other settings.

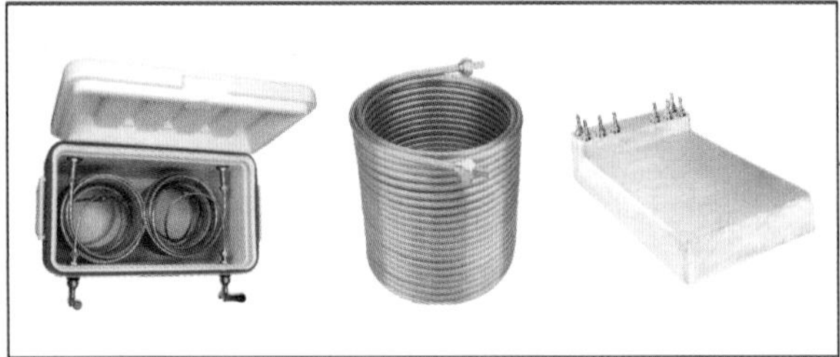

**Figure 2.2.** *Left to right:* A typical jockey box system equipped with coils, a stainless steel coil, and a cold plate.

## JOCKEY BOX SETUP AND USE

A coil has a relatively high surface area to volume ratio when compared to a cold plate, because the length of tubing that the beer passes through in a coil is greater. This means coil-style jockey boxes can pour chilled beer at a faster rate than those equipped with a cold plate. Thus, coil-style jockey boxes are better suited for situations where faster pour rates and greater volumes are needed. With a lower surface area for chilling, the cold plate style is appropriate when the beer can be dispensed more slowly.

Kegs used with a cold plate jockey box should be iced if the ambient temperature is above 55°F since the plate has a limited cooling capacity. By constrast, a coil-style jockey box can pour beer efficiently even with the kegs sitting at room temperature (64–74°F). If the ambient temperature is above room temperature, the kegs should be iced even when using a coil-style jockey box.

Beer line used with a jockey box should be colored since the line is typically subjected to light, which has the potential to cause light-struck beer. This is the ONLY time where flexible vinyl beer line is suggested to be dark. It does not allow for a visual inspection and so should be clear in all other situations.

### Setting Up a Cold Plate Jockey Box

- Tap the keg and run beer through the faucet before adding ice to the jockey box. This removes water left behind during the cleaning process before temperatures in the plate get cold enough to freeze it, causing turbulence or blockage of the beer flow.
- Place ice both underneath and on top of the cold plate in the ice chest. As time passes, the ice will "bridge" and should be removed to allow better contact with the cold plate and remaining ice. Ice should be added periodically and water drained from the ice chest.
- Set $CO_2$ pressure at 25 to 35 psi. This will vary depending on how much tubing is contained in the plate and thus how much resistance to flow is built into each line. Pressure can be adjusted to attain desired flow rate.

### Setting Up a Coil-Style Jockey Box

- Tap the keg and run beer through the coil and out the faucet.
- Add ice to the ice chest and completely cover the coil.
- Add cold water to the top of the coil. This creates an ice bath, giving excellent surface contact. Ice water is also a better heat conductor than straight ice.
- Set $CO_2$ pressure at 35 to 40 psi on 120 ft. coils. Shorter coils are not recommended but, if used, should dispense beer at 30 to 35 psi. Since coil length varies, so too will psi. This is usually a trial and error process as opposed to an actual calculation.

## DRAUGHT SAFETY

When not in use, all beer lines should be left clean and pH neutral (i.e., all cleaning chemicals thoroughly rinsed away). The lines should be blown out with $CO_2$ or hung up vertically to air dry, if possible.

### CLEANING AND MAINTENANCE

Temporary dispensing equipment must be cleaned immediately after use. It is nearly impossible to remove the mold and biofilms that can result from storing cold plates, coils, or a jockey box that has had old beer left in the lines.

For cleaning jockey boxes, refer to the detailed electric cleaning pump procedures outlined in chapter 7. After cleaning, the water in the lines must be blown out to prevent mold growth and preferably hung up vertically to remain dry.

- If the recirculation pump is capable of being run dry: before breaking down the recirculation loop, remove the inlet from the rinse water with the pump running so air pushes out all of the rinse water in the lines.
- If the recirculation pump is *not* capable of being run dry: after breaking down the recirculation loop and reattaching faucets, tap an empty **pressure pot**, or **cleaning canister**, and use the gas pressure to blow all of the water out of the lines.

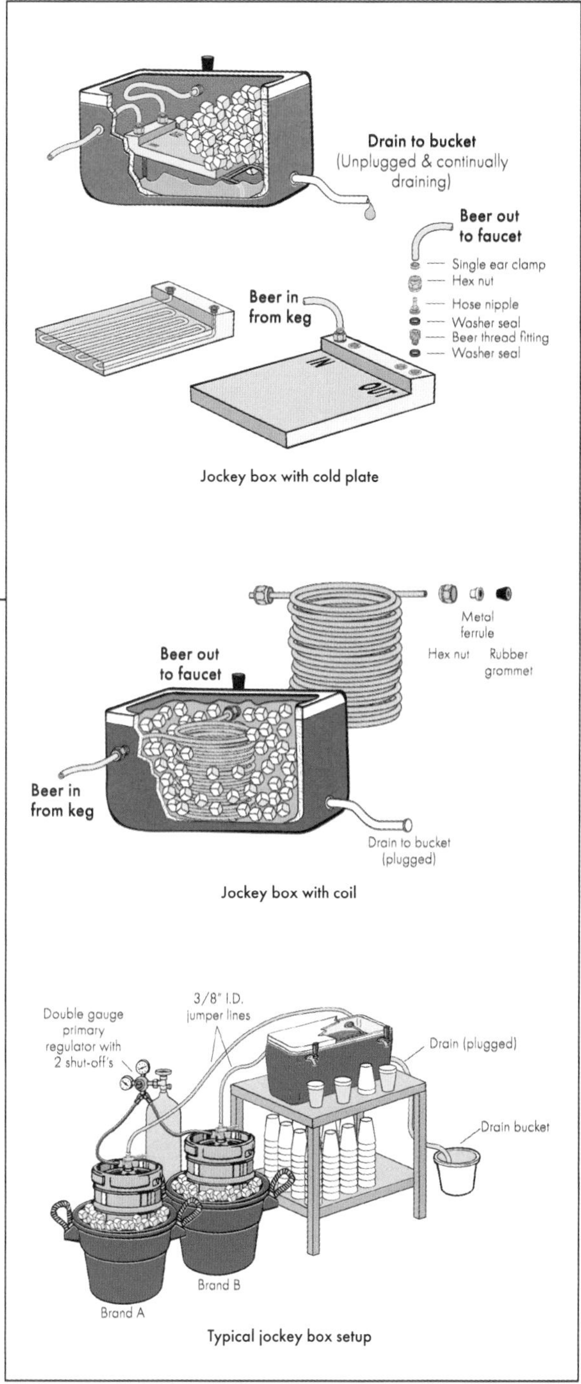


**Figure 2.3.** Water should be allowed to drain out of the jockey box when using a cold plate. A coil should be submerged in ice water during use.

3

# DIRECT-DRAW DRAUGHT SYSTEMS

Retailers use direct-draw systems in situations where the kegs can be kept refrigerated in very close proximity to the dispensing point or faucet. In some cases, the beer sits in a cooler below the counter at the bar. This is a **keg box**, or **kegerator**, a self-contained refrigerator where the number of kegs accommodated varies based on box and keg size. The other common direct-draw system is a walk-in cooler that shares a wall with the bar, keeping the kegs close to the dispensing point so that beer can be drawn directly through the wall from the keg to the faucet.

**Figure 3.1.** Common direct-draw systems, a keg box *(left)* and walk-in cooler *(right)*.

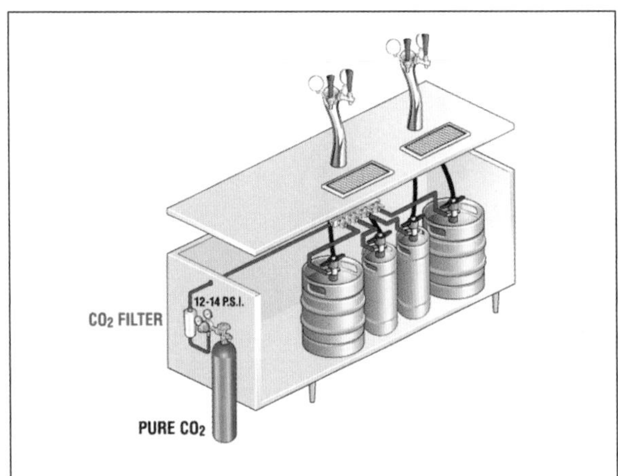


**Figure 3.2.** A typical direct-draw system.

## EQUIPMENT

The nine components discussed in chapter 1 appear in both types of direct-draw system; only a little additional equipment comes into play. As with temporary systems like jockey boxes, most direct-draw systems employ vinyl tubing, or other flexible tubing, and pure $CO_2$ gas. Compared to barrier tubing, vinyl beer line is relatively permeable to oxygen ingress and the flavor of beer stored in these lines can change overnight. As part of their opening procedures each day, some retailers will drain this beer or, in some cases, use it for cooking. A newer generation of flexible tubing has become available in recent years that, in some instances, demonstrates barrier-like qualities, including both a lower permeability to oxygen ingress and lower likelihood of flavor absorption.

As permanent installations, direct-draw systems typically include a drip tray and some systems also incorporate a tap tower. In addition, shanks support the faucets in either tower or wall-mount applications. The following sections discuss these elements of the system, as well as the use of $CO_2$.

### Drip Tray

Many draught systems include a drip tray placed below the faucets and most health departments require them (fig. 3.3).

Many walk-in based direct-draw systems use a wall-mounted drip tray that includes a backsplash. This design may be used on some air-cooled long-draw systems as well. Bars typically place surface or recessed drip trays under draught towers. Many of these will also include a glass rinser for prerinsing clean glasses. These drip trays should be plumbed to empty into a drain or floor sink.

**Figure 3.3.** Common drip tray setups. *Top to bottom*: wall-mounted with backsplash, surface-mounted under faucets with rinser.

Photo © Getty/EddieHernandezPhotography (wall mounted faucets)

### Towers

Direct-draw keg boxes and most long-draw systems mount the dispensing faucet on a tower. This tower attaches to the top of the bar or keg box. Towers come in various shapes and sizes and may have anywhere from one to dozens of faucets (fig. 3.4).

To achieve proper beer service, the beer line running through the tower to the faucet must be kept at the same temperature as the beer cooler. Direct-draw systems use air cooling, while long-draw systems typically use glycol cooling. Air-cooled towers are insulated on the inside and cold air from the cooler circulates around the beer lines and shanks. This works with direct-draw systems thanks to the close proximity of the tower to the walk-in cooler. Some keg boxes have specialized corrugated tubing connected to the refrigerator's evaporator housing. This tubing is designed to be inserted in the tower to provide for cold air flow up to the faucet. Typically, cold air is supplied directly from the discharge of the evaporator and is colder than the keg temperature.

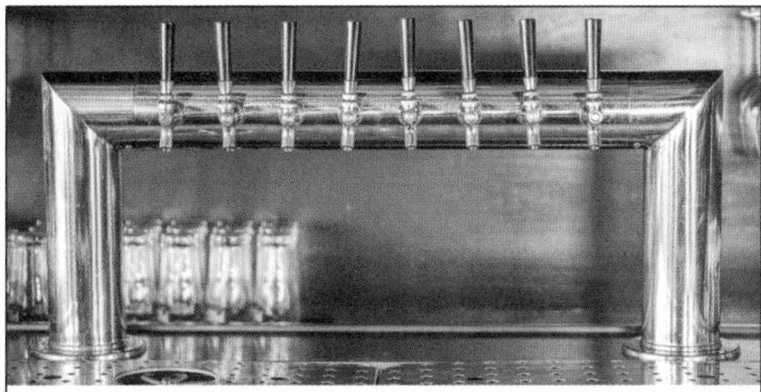

**Figure 3.4.** A pass-through tower with eight faucets *(top)* and a double faucet tower *(bottom)*.

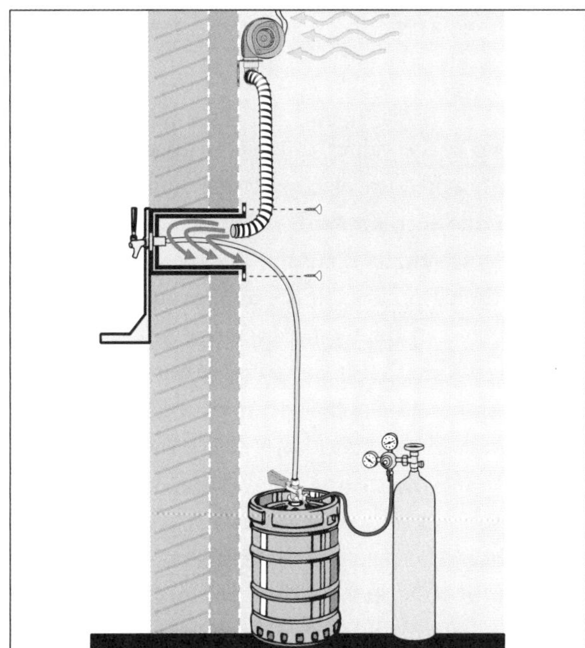

**Figure 3.5.** Shadow box.

### Shadow Box

In some direct-draw applications that use a walk-in cooler, it may be necessary to cut a section out of the cooler wall where the shanks are placed (fig. 3.5). The wall is then recessed in a **shadow box** to minimize the shank length and keep foaming to a minimum.

### Gas ($CO_2$)

$CO_2$ is the primary gas used to dispense draught beer. $CO_2$ in the head space of the keg or serving tank serves to maintain proper carbonation within the beer and also provides pressure to help move the beer from the cooler through the beer lines to the faucet. $CO_2$ used for dispensing beverages must be of sufficient purity and free of off-aromas and organic or other contaminants. See appendix A for detailed purity specifications.

## DRAUGHT SAFETY

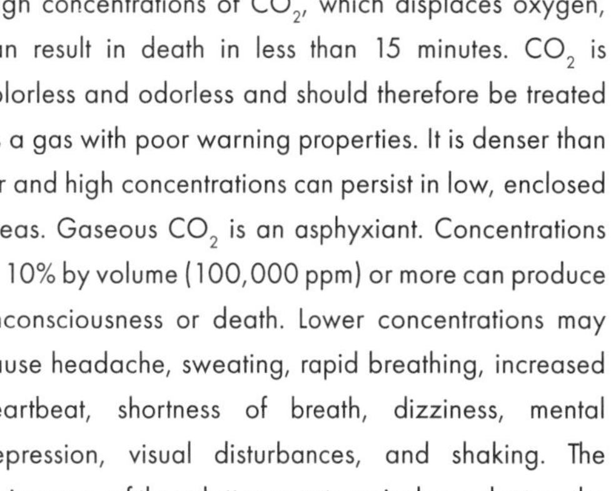

High concentrations of $CO_2$, which displaces oxygen, can result in death in less than 15 minutes. $CO_2$ is colorless and odorless and should therefore be treated as a gas with poor warning properties. It is denser than air and high concentrations can persist in low, enclosed areas. Gaseous $CO_2$ is an asphyxiant. Concentrations of 10% by volume (100,000 ppm) or more can produce unconsciousness or death. Lower concentrations may cause headache, sweating, rapid breathing, increased heartbeat, shortness of breath, dizziness, mental depression, visual disturbances, and shaking. The seriousness of these latter symptoms is dependent on the $CO_2$ concentration and the length of time the individual is exposed. The response to $CO_2$ inhalation varies greatly between individuals.

$CO_2$ Monitors

Electronic $CO_2$ monitors are available for installation in walk-in coolers. Such devices can prevent serious injury or death from $CO_2$ inhalation by sounding an alarm when $CO_2$ levels are elevated.

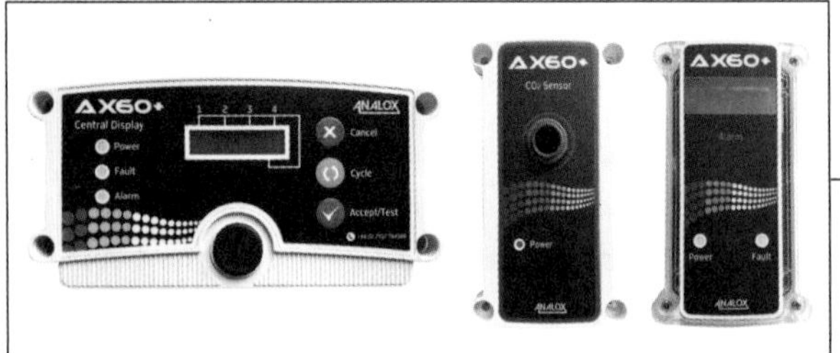


**Figure 3.6.** Electronic carbon dioxide ($CO_2$) monitor and alarm.

## DRAUGHT SAFETY

Good general ventilation should be sufficient to control worker exposure. Carbon dioxide detection devices should be installed and regularly inspected in enclosed environments such as walk-in coolers and storage rooms. Personal $CO_2$ or oxygen monitors can help workers to be aware of any asphyxiation hazards.

While performing maintenance on any system involving $CO_2$, the gas should be shut off prior to any work being performed. If $CO_2$ is released inside an enclosed environment it should be immediately ventilated to allow $CO_2$ levels to return to normal. Anyone working in such an environment should avoid working in low points where $CO_2$ accumulates.

### CARBONATION DYNAMICS

The level of carbonation in beer responds to changes in storage and serving conditions. Let's consider an average keg with a carbonation of 2.5 volumes of $CO_2$ (see Units of Carbonation sidebar) and see what happens when conditions change.

For any keg, the beer temperature and the $CO_2$ pressure applied to the keg influences the amount of $CO_2$ that is dissolved in the beer (table 3.1). At a given temperature, a specific pressure must be applied to the keg to maintain the carbonation established by the brewery. If temperature or pressure varies, carbonation levels will change.

## UNITS OF CARBONATION

In the United States and some other countries, the industry measures beer carbonation in units of "volumes of $CO_2$." A typical value for a keg might be 2.5 volumes of $CO_2$, meaning literally that 2.5 keg-volumes of uncompressed $CO_2$ has been compressed and dissolved into one keg of beer. Carbonation levels in typical beers run from 2.2 to 2.8 volumes of $CO_2$ but values can range from as little as 1.2 to as high as 4.0 in specialty beers.

In Europe and other countries, the industry typically measures carbonation in terms of "grams per $CO_2$ per liter of beer." A good rule of thumb is to multiply volumes of $CO_2$ by 2 to estimate grams per liter. So, a beer with 2.5 volumes of $CO_2$ would contain about 5 grams per liter of $CO_2$. For more information on this calculation, see appendix B.

**TABLE 3.1.** BEER CARBONATION AT SEA LEVEL IN VOLUMES $CO_2$ AS A FUNCTION OF SYSTEM TEMPERATURE AND $CO_2$ PRESSURE*

| | $CO_2$ pressure (psi) | | |
|---|---|---|---|
| **Temp (°F)** | **9** | **11** | **13** |
| **34** | 2.5 | 2.7 | 2.9 |
| **38** | 2.3 | 2.5 | 2.7 |
| **42** | 2.1 | 2.3 | 2.5 |

*Pressures rounded for purposes of illustration. Do not use this table for system adjustment.

Looking at the values in table 3.1, beer in a keg at 38°F needs a pressure of 11 psi to maintain 2.5 volumes of $CO_2$ as the beer is served. As long as the temperature and pressure remain constant, the beer maintains the same carbonation level. If the temperature of the beer changes, so does the required internal keg pressure. In table 3.1, we see that if the pressure remains at 11 psi but the temperature of the beer rises to 42°F, the overall carbonation in the beer drops to 2.3 volumes of $CO_2$ (this drop may occur over a few days). This is because $CO_2$ dissolved in the beer moves from the beer to the head space. Alternately, if the temperature remains at 38°F but the $CO_2$ pressure increases to 13 psi, then the carbonation level of the beer in the keg will increase to 2.7 volumes as the beer absorbs additional $CO_2$.

The **ideal gauge pressure** for a beer is the pressure at which $CO_2$ is not diffusing from beer into the head space and excess $CO_2$ is not absorbing in the beer. This value varies from location to location depending upon factors such as temperature, altitude, and carbonation level of the beer. Because beer carbonation can vary with the temperature of your cooler and the pressure applied to the keg, you must take care to maintain steady values suited to your system and beers.

**Figure 3.7.** A secondary regulator is used to adjust individual keg pressure to the ideal gauge pressure appropriate for the system and beer.

### A Note about Altitude

Pressure gauges used on draught systems measure in pounds per square inch, gauge (psig). This is the difference between the pressure in the keg and atmospheric pressure (atmospheric pressure is 14.7 psi at sea level). When dispensing beer at higher elevations, the carbonation level of the beer does not change but the pressure displayed on the gauge (i.e., psig) will read low, by approximately 1 psi per every 2000 feet of elevation. So a keg dispensed at 10,000 feet would need to have the gauge pressure increased by approximately 5 psig above the calculated dispensing pressure at sea level. See page 18 in chapter 1 for more details on correcting for elevation.

## DETERMINING $CO_2$ PRESSURE IN A DIRECT-DRAW SYSTEM

Because direct-draw systems are typically quite short, the pressure of pure (100%) $CO_2$ required to maintain proper carbonation is usually sufficient by itself to also deliver the beer from the keg to the faucet without overcarbonating the beer.

You can determine ideal gauge pressure for pure $CO_2$ using table 3.2 (reproduced in appendix B). If you do not know the carbonation level in the beer, you can estimate it using the procedure found in appendix B.

## SYSTEM BALANCE AND ACHIEVING FLOW

So far we have seen what happens to a beer's carbonation in the keg as the result of applied pressure and temperature. Beer must travel from the keg to the glass, and along the way it encounters an opposing force, **resistance**. The beer line and changes in height impart resistance to the flow of beer from the keg to the faucet. The pressure applied to the keg overcomes this resistance and drives the beer through the system and to the customer's glass. To achieve proper flow and beer quality, the pressure applied to the keg must equal the total resistance of the draught system.

**Figure 3.8.** Properly balanced draught dispensing systems should deliver beer with a proper head.

We have already demonstrated that the pressure applied to the keg needs to be matched to the carbonation level of the beer. This creates a problem when the resistance of the system calls for more (or less) pressure than is needed to maintain the carbonation of the beer. To prevent conflicts and to balance the system, draught technicians design system resistance to match the pressure applied to the beer.

A balanced draught dispensing system delivers clear-pouring beer at the rate of two ounces per second. This means it takes about eight seconds to fill a pint glass and about one minute to pour one gallon of beer.

For most direct-draw systems, balancing the system is quite simple. Most direct-draw kegerators and walk-in coolers where the kegs are close to the faucets will simply take a 4–5 ft. length of 3/16" internal diameter (ID) vinyl tubing (*see* table 3.3).

Some system setups benefit from flow rates faster or slower than 1 gal./min. If you try to achieve faster pours by increasing the gas pressure, you will create

Photos © Aaron Colussi (regulator); Christine Celmins Photography (beer)

**TABLE 3.2.** DETERMINATION OF PURE $CO_2$ EQUILIBRIUM GAUGE PRESSURE (PSIG) FOR GIVEN VOLUMES OF $CO_2$ AND TEMPERATURE

| | Volumes of $CO_2$ | | | | | | | | | | |
|---|---|---|---|---|---|---|---|---|---|---|---|
| **Temp. (°F)** | **2.1** | **2.2** | **2.3** | **2.4** | **2.5** | **2.6** | **2.7** | **2.8** | **2.9** | **3.0** | **3.1** |
| **33** | 5.0 | 6.0 | 6.9 | 7.9 | 8.8 | 9.8 | 10.7 | 11.7 | 12.6 | 13.6 | 14.5 |
| **34** | 5.2 | 6.2 | 7.2 | 8.1 | 9.1 | 10.1 | 11.1 | 12.0 | 13.0 | 14.0 | 15.0 |
| **35** | 5.6 | 6.6 | 7.6 | 8.6 | 9.7 | 10.7 | 11.7 | 12.7 | 13.7 | 14.8 | 15.8 |
| **36** | 6.1 | 7.1 | 8.2 | 9.2 | 10.2 | 11.3 | 12.3 | 13.4 | 14.4 | 15.5 | 16.5 |
| **37** | 6.6 | 7.6 | 8.7 | 9.8 | 10.8 | 11.9 | 12.9 | 14.0 | 15.1 | 16.1 | 17.2 |
| **38** | 7.0 | 8.1 | 9.2 | 10.3 | 11.3 | 12.4 | 13.5 | 14.5 | 15.6 | 16.7 | 17.8 |
| **39** | 7.6 | 8.7 | 9.8 | 10.8 | 11.9 | 13.0 | 14.1 | 15.2 | 16.3 | 17.4 | 18.5 |
| **40** | 8.0 | 9.1 | 10.2 | 11.3 | 12.4 | 13.5 | 14.6 | 15.7 | 16.8 | 17.9 | 19.0 |
| **41** | 8.3 | 9.4 | 10.6 | 11.7 | 12.8 | 13.9 | 15.1 | 16.2 | 17.3 | 18.4 | 19.5 |
| **42** | 8.8 | 9.9 | 11.0 | 12.2 | 13.3 | 14.4 | 15.6 | 16.7 | 17.8 | 19.0 | 20.1 |

**Source:** Data from *Methods of Analysis*, 5th ed. (Milwaukee, WI: American Society of Brewing Chemists, 1949).
**Note:** Values assume sea-level altitude. Add 1 psi for every 2000 ft. above sea level.

overcarbonated beer and foam at the tap. Foamy beer can also result if you try to achieve slower pours by decreasing the gas pressure; this can also create flat beer. If you need to change flow rate, the resistance of the system should be altered to achieve the desired result, not the gas pressure. Gas pressure, once set for a particular beer, remains constant and should never be adjusted to alter the flow rate of the beer.

For long-draw systems or systems that need different flow rates, figuring restriction and choosing the correct tubing is more complex. For more information on these calculations, see Appendix C. ■

**Figure 3.9.** Direct-draw kegerator with single tower.

**TABLE 3.3.** DIRECT-DRAW DRAUGHT SYSTEM BALANCE AT 38°F

| **Carbonation (volumes $CO_2$)** | 2.3 | 2.4 | 2.5 | 2.6 | 2.7 | 2.8 | 2.9 |
|---|---|---|---|---|---|---|---|
| **Applied $CO_2$ (psig)** | 9.2 | 10.3 | 11.3 | 12.4 | 13.5 | 14.5 | 15.6 |
| **3/16" Vinyl beer line length** | 3'3" | 3'5" | 3'9" | 4'2" | 4'6" | 4'10" | 5'7" |

4

# LONG-DRAW DRAUGHT SYSTEMS

The most complex draught systems fall into the long-draw category. Designed to deliver beer to bars well away from the keg cooler, long-draw systems usually employ equipment not seen in temporary and direct-draw setups. From around 1990 to 2010, the average long-draw system doubled in complexity from roughly five faucets to more than 10 faucets. Today it is common to find very complex draught systems at retail with dozens of faucets. While long-draw systems offer designers the option to put beer far from the bar, allowing more flexibility with keg handling or layout, the distances they cover can cause problems and increase costs for equipment, cooling, and beer waste. As with all systems, it is important to minimize line length and diameter where possible to reduce beer loss and facilitate cleaning.

Here we will consider long-draw systems by focusing on the three main components of a draught dispensing system: beer line, gas, and cooling.

## BEER LINE

While exceptions exist, most long-draw systems still push beer from kegs. Beer exits the keg through a coupler and usually enters a vinyl or other flexible beer line, just as we have seen with temporary and direct-draw systems. But in long-draw systems the flexible tubing does not last long. It typically goes about six feet before connecting to a wall bracket that serves as a transition to specialized barrier tubing. Designed for minimum resistance and superior cleanliness, barrier tubing should carry beer most of the distance from keg to faucet in long-draw systems. Barrier tubing is not the end of the journey;

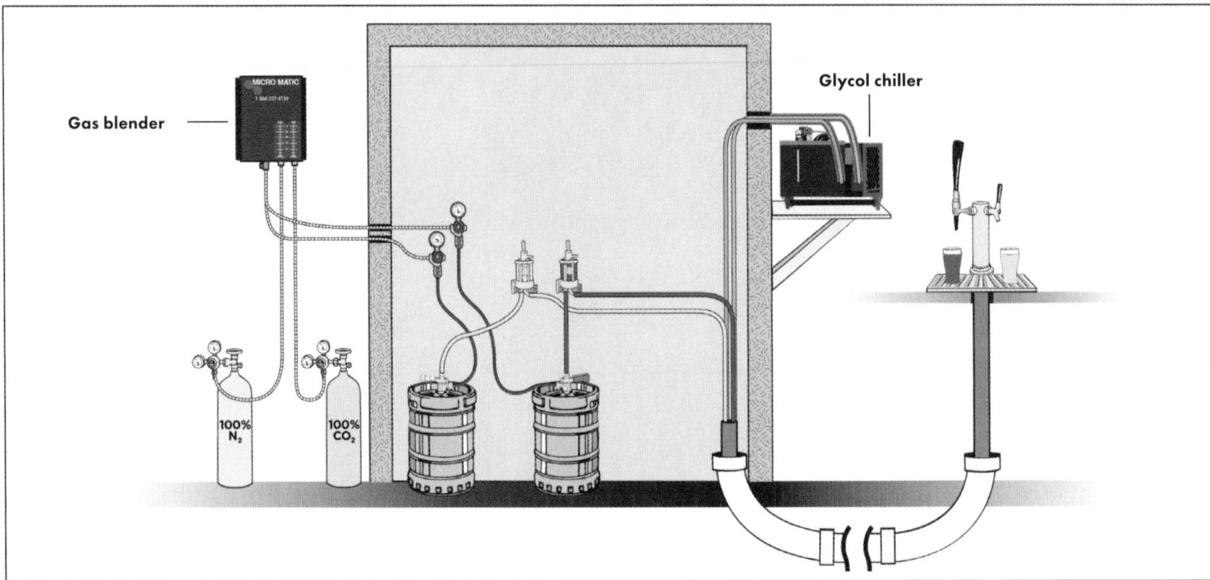


**Figure 4.1.** Configuration of a typical long-draw system.

most draught towers use stainless steel tubing to carry the beer to the faucet. In addition, many systems include some length of narrow-gauge vinyl or other flexible tubing, called **choker line**, between the end of the barrier tubing and the stainless steel tubing of the draught tower, which provides a way to accurately balance the system. In the end, however, the beer flows through a faucet just as we saw with the direct-draw systems.

You may also find foam on beer detectors (usually referred to as **FOBs**) on the beer lines of many long-draw systems. Located in the cooler at or near the wall bracket, these devices fill with dispensing gas when beer from a keg runs out, thereby shutting off flow to the main beer line. This prevents beer loss by keeping the main beer line full of pressurized beer while the keg is changed. The jumper line between the keg and FOB is then purged and normal beer service can resume. FOBs are discussed in further detail later on in this chapter.

### Barrier Tubing

Barrier tubing has a "glass-smooth" lining that inhibits beer or mineral stone deposits and also inhibits microbial growth to maintain beer freshness. Its properties make barrier tubing the only industry-approved beer line for long-draw systems.

Barrier tubing may be purchased separately in various diameters, but most suppliers sell it in prepared bundles (called bundle or trunk housing) that have beer lines and glycol coolant lines wrapped inside an insulating cover (fig. 4.2). These bundles vary by the number of beer lines they carry, with popular sizes matching the number of faucets commonly found on tap towers.

Many older long-draw systems have single-wall polyethylene tubing installed. This relatively porous

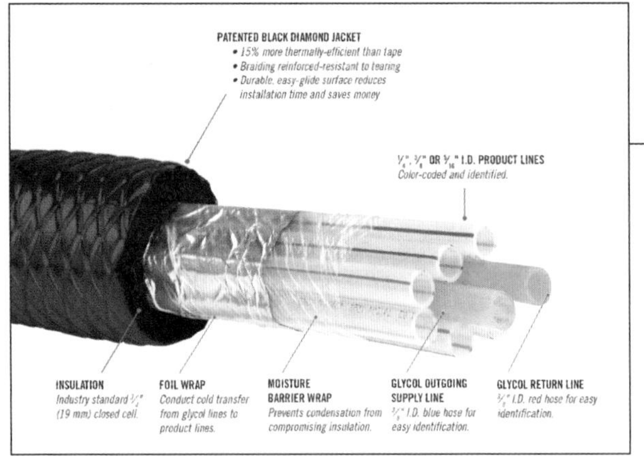


**Figure 4.2.** Cross-section of a long-draw beer line bundle.

material allows oxygen to enter, $CO_2$ to escape, and makes cleaning difficult, resulting in stale, flat, and potentially tainted beer in the lines. Older long-draw systems with vinyl or polyethylene beer lines should be repacked with fresh beer each day because of the detrimental effects of oxidation (the beer drained during this process can be used for cooking, however). This expense alone can significantly decrease the payback time when replacing beer lines in an old long-draw system with barrier tubing.

Today, you may find blue and red polyethylene tubing carrying glycol from and to your glycol power pack—this is the only recommended use for polyethylene tubing in long-draw systems. Vinyl tubing should only be used as jumper line between keg couplers and long-draw barrier tubing trunks, and avoided wherever possible as choker line between barrier tubing trunks and faucet shanks (discussed in the next section). Vinyl and polyethylene tubing should never be used in long-draw bundles.

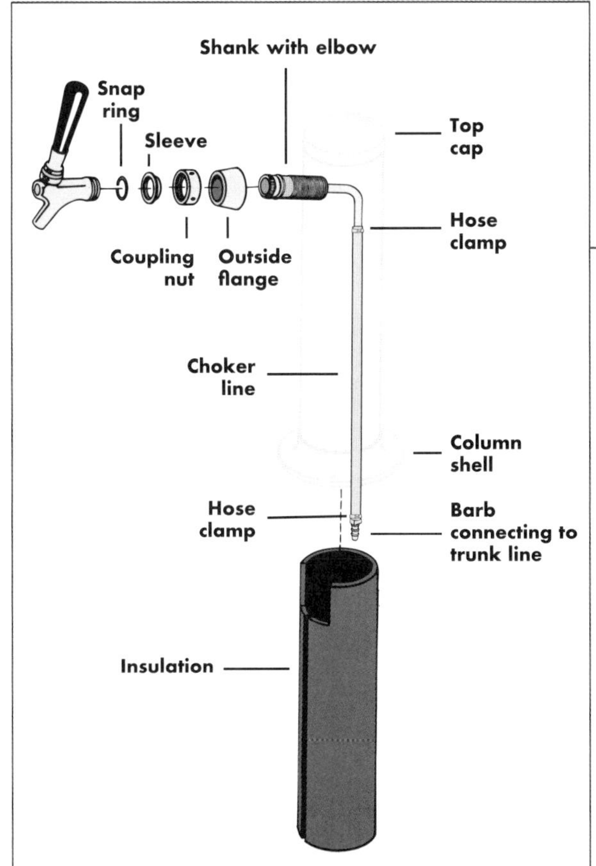


**Figure 4.3.** Choker line within faucet tower.

### Choker Line

Choker line, also known as restriction tubing, is a section of 3⁄16" ID vinyl or flexible tubing of variable length installed at the tower end of a long-draw system (fig. 4.3). The purpose is to add to the overall system restriction and thus achieve the target flow rate at the faucet. Choker line is connected at one end to the barrier tubing in the trunk housing with a reducing splicer, and at the other end to a hose barb on either the back side of the shank inside the tower or to the stainless tubing extending from the tower.

Wherever possible, vinyl tubing should not be used as choker tubing between barrier tubing bundles and faucet shanks. In this more permanent application, vinyl tubing is very difficult to regularly replace. Alternatives to vinyl should be explored, which might include using alternative, higher-quality flexible tubing or other means of adding resistance. See the "System Balance and Achieving Flow" section below for more information.

### Wall Brackets

Wall brackets join tubing together in a long-draw walk-in cooler. The wall bracket gives a solid connecting spot for jumper lines from the keg. Tubing is connected with a washer, nut, tail piece, and clamp combination.

Most wall brackets installed in the past were made of plated brass, which should be inspected for wear and replaced with stainless steel.

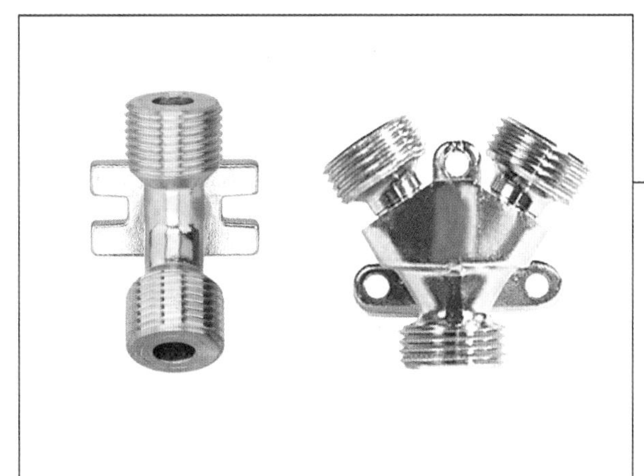

**Figure 4.4.** One-faucet bracket *(left)* and two-faucet wall bracket *(right)*.

## Foam on Beer Detector (FOB)

An FOB stops the flow of beer through a line once the keg empties. This reduces the beer loss normally associated with changing a keg and therefore reduces operating costs. While available in different designs, most FOBs feature a float in a sealed bowl that drops when beer flow from the keg stops, which allows the beer lines to stay packed.

FOBs should be cleaned every two weeks when the draught system is cleaned. They should also be completely disassembled and manually cleaned every six months to ensure a clean system.

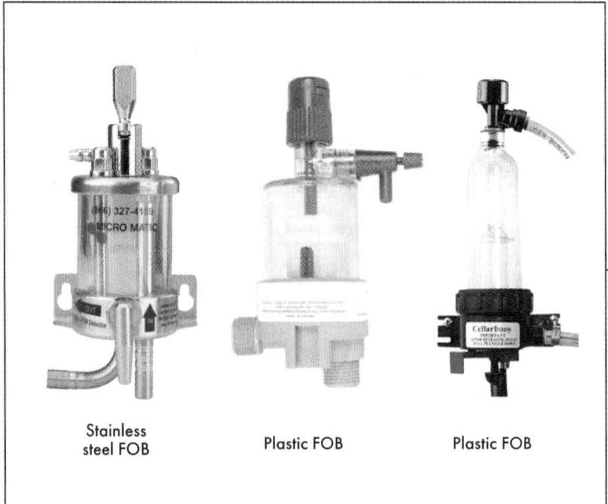


**Figure 4.5.** Stainless steel FOB *(left)* and two types of plastic FOB *(middle and right)*.

## Beer Pumps

**Beer pumps** draw beer from a keg or other beer serving vessel and deliver it to the faucet. Rather than using gas pressure to drive beer, beer pumps use mechanical force to propel the beer through the system. Beer pumps are usually found in draught systems when working pressures for gas-driven dispense get too high (above 35 or 40 psi), which includes very long runs (>200 feet) or high vertical **lifts**. Above these pressures, beer will absorb enough nitrogen from the blended dispensing gas to create long-lasting, smaller-sized foam bubbles that in turn can cause problems when dispensing beer. Beer pumps are often used on multibarrel brewpub serving tanks that have low-pressure limits. Serving tanks must be constructed to American Society of Mechanical Engineers (ASME) standards in order to safely dispense beer above 15 psi.

Beer pumps themselves are powered by high-pressure gas or compressed air that does not come into contact with the beer. Most retailers power their beer pumps with $CO_2$; in these cases, the pump exhaust $CO_2$ gas must be vented outside the cooler or building to avoid $CO_2$ buildup and asphyxiation. Carbon dioxide can be relatively expensive to use to power beer pumps compared to compressed air, but $CO_2$ is usually already available at any location serving draught beer, so is often simpler to use.

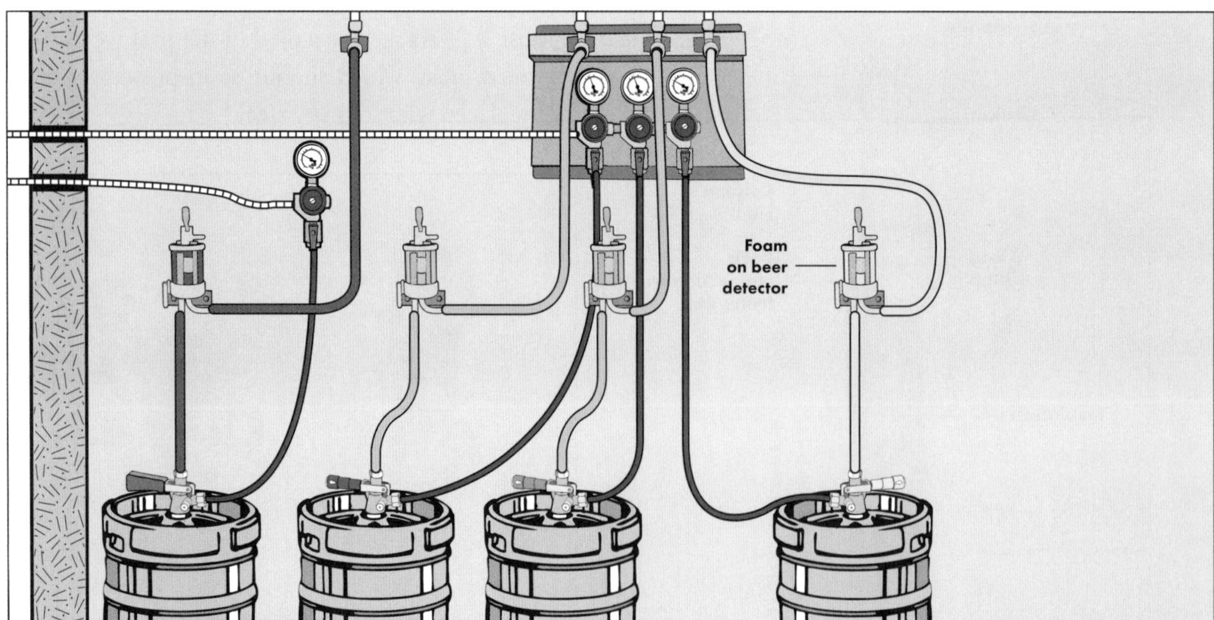


**Figure 4.6.** FOBs and wall brackets in walk-in cooler.

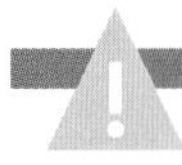

## DRAUGHT SAFETY

The exhaust $CO_2$ gas from a beer pump must be vented outside the walk-in cooler or building to avoid $CO_2$ buildup and asphyxiation.

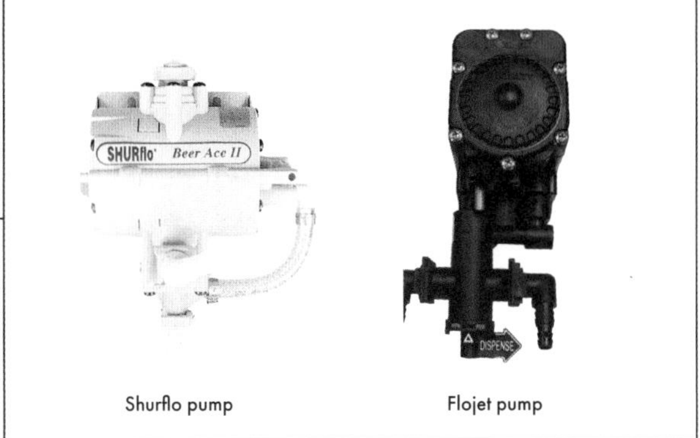


**Figure 4.7.** Examples of beer pumps: a SHURflo® pump *(left)* and a Flojet® pump *(right)*.

If using compressed air to drive beer pumps, pump and keg regulators must be separated—compressed air should never come into contact with draught beer. Also, high-quality air compressors that clean and dry the air must be used to avoid damaging beer pumps. Smaller, less expensive air compressors may deliver air with small amounts of moisture or oil that can damage beer pumps over time and they can break down, leaving the retailer unable to dispense beer.

Some portion of the pump contacts the beer and, like anything else, it must be regularly cleaned to prevent **beer stone** buildup and microbial contamination. See special cleaning considerations on page 74 of this manual.

Beer pump setups require two operational pressures: $CO_2$ pressure on the keg or tank to maintain beer carbonation, and separate gas pressure to the pump so that the pump can propel beer to the faucet. There are two basic beer pump types, fixed pressure and additive pressure. Fixed pressure pumps are becoming much less common today. Because fixed pressure pumps deliver beer at the same pressure being applied to the beer keg or tank, they are less useful in systems balanced at higher pressures. Additive pressure beer pumps are most useful for very long long-draw systems, since the pressure applied to the keg is added to the pressure of the gas driving the beer pump. Additive pressure pumps have one other advantage—beer may still be dispensed (although much more slowly) if they fail, whereas beer cannot be served if a fixed pressure pump fails.

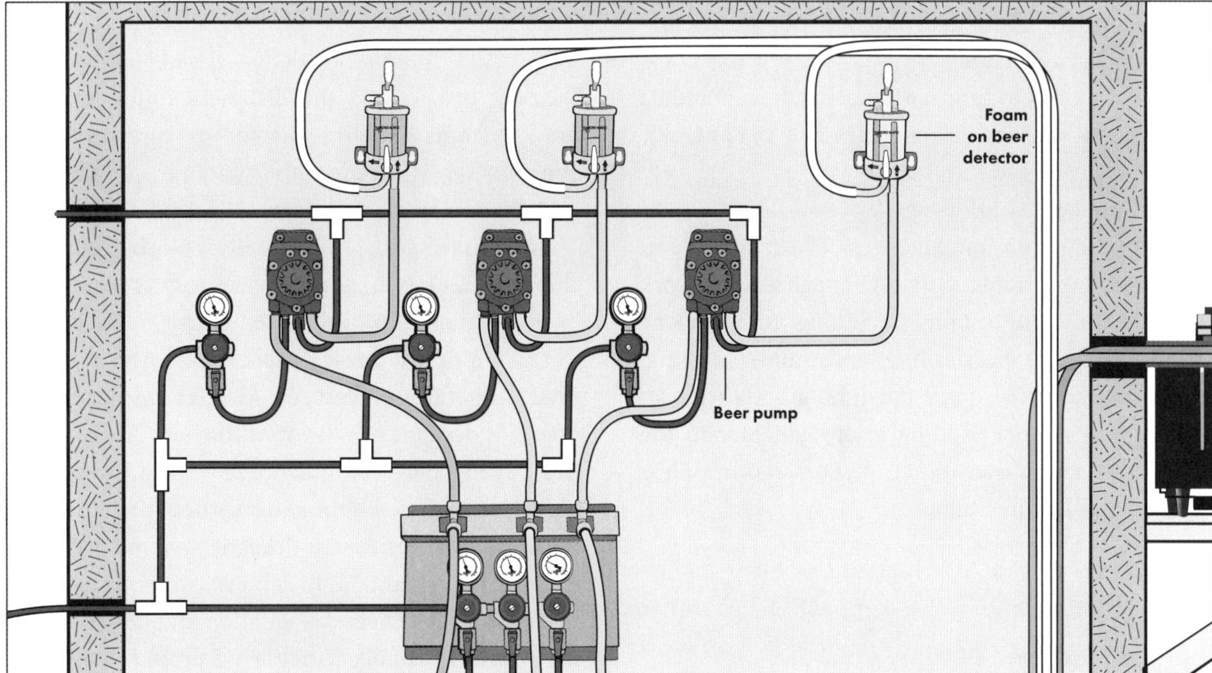


**Figure 4.8.** Beer pumps and FOBs in walk-in cooler.

Here are some good rules of thumb for using beer pumps in draught beer dispensing systems:

- Be sure to refer to detailed cleaning procedures provided by the pump manufacturer, and to procedures found on page 74 of this manual. Do not let your cleaning solution get too hot or you will damage your pump.
- Only use beer pumps that come fitted with a diverter or backflush fitting, so the pump can be properly cleaned using recirculation pumps in either forward or backward direction.
- Proper $CO_2$ pressure (ideal gauge pressure) should be applied to the keg or tank to maintain the beer's carbonation level (see appendix B).
- When using additive pressure-type pumps, set pump pressure so that the sum total of the keg pressure plus pump pressure together equal system resistance pressure.
- Draught systems that utilize beer pumps should have FOBs placed immediately after the pump. This keeps the pump from running dry when the beer supply to the pump runs out, a primary cause of pump failure.
- Vent beer pump exhaust $CO_2$ out of the walk-in cooler or building.
- Don't run more than two faucets per beer pump.
- Don't run more than two beer pumps per secondary regulator.
- For pumps to function properly, they should be located close to the source (i.e., the keg or tank).

### Quick-Connect (Push) Fittings

Special fittings can join all types of beer line found in long-draw systems. Quick-connect fittings work on hard or rigid tubing, including polyethylene (used for glycol), barrier line, and stainless tubing. Couplers attach to square-cut tubing ends with an O-ring and gripper. Adding a vinyl adapter to the coupler allows for transition from barrier or stainless steel to vinyl/flexible tubing.

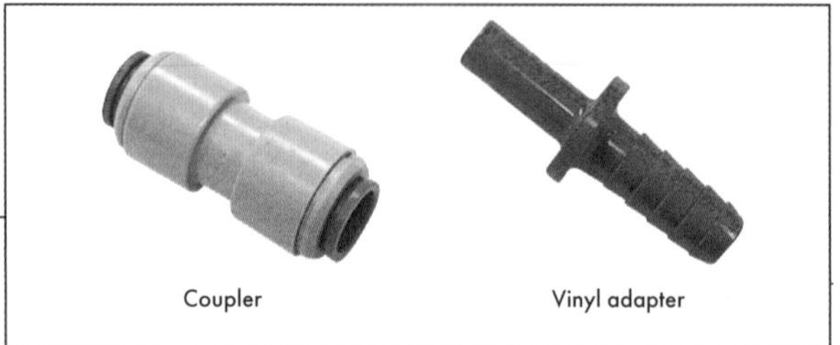


**Figure 4.9.** Examples of quick-connect fittings.

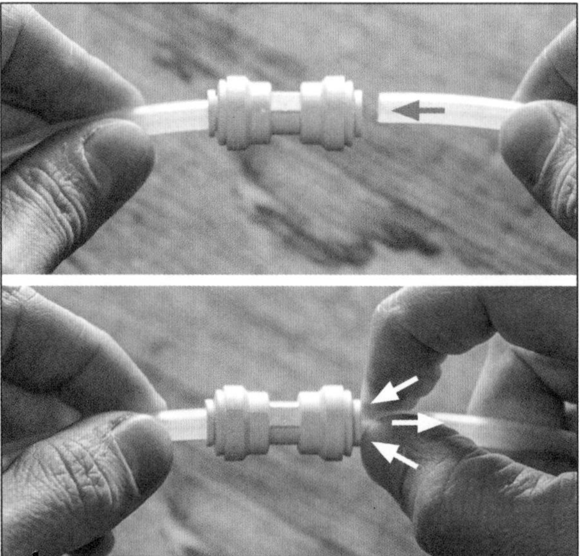

**Figure 4.10.** Tubing can simply be inserted into quick-connect fittings to make a connection. For removal, a collet must be depressed as the hose is pulled out of the fitting.

## GAS

### Mixed Gas: Carbon Dioxide ($CO_2$) and Nitrogen ($N_2$)

Pushing beer across the distances found in long-draw systems usually calls for gas pressures well above what is needed to maintain proper beer carbonation levels with pure (100%) $CO_2$.

As we have seen, beer readily absorbs $CO_2$. Any change in $CO_2$ pressure on a beer results in a change in the carbonation of the beer. Nitrogen ($N_2$) is different. For one, it does not absorb into beer at typical system operating pressures. Also, as an inert gas, it does not degrade the flavor of the beer. These qualities make $N_2$ perfect for blending with $CO_2$ to achieve higher pressures without overcarbonating the beer. Thus, in high-resistance draught systems, we use a mixture of $CO_2$ and $N_2$ to achieve two objectives: (1) maintain proper beer carbonation and (2) overcome the system resistance to achieve a proper pour.

## PURE $CO_2$ AND LONG-DRAW SYSTEMS

Pure (100%) $CO_2$ should only be used in a long-draw system in very specific situations. One of these situations is in a beer pump system, as described on pg. 32. In the absence of a beer pump, the following conditions must be met: (1) ideal gauge pressure is sufficient to produce the proper flow rate and (2) there is absolutely no temperature increase in the beer lines outside the cooler, both conditions which are highly unlikely. Since ideal gauge pressure with 100% $CO_2$ is relatively low, even a slight temperature increase from the keg cooler to the draught line can allow the $CO_2$ to escape from the beer in the beer line, causing foamy beer at the tap. The higher pressure of blended gas can to some degree help eliminate foaming caused by a temperature increase by keeping beer packed several pounds above the carbonation breakout pressure.

Calculating the exact mix of $CO_2$ and $N_2$ depends on all the factors we have discussed: beer temperature and carbonation, system resistance, and the total applied pressure that's required to maintain the carbonation of the beer. The details of these calculations are shown in appendix C. There are also some excellent resources online, including easy-to-use calculators to help determine the exact custom blend needed for your draught system (see mcdantim.com for calculators or download the McDantim EasyBlend Calculator app, *see* fig 4.18).

The correct blend can be purchased premixed in blended gas bottles, or custom blends can be mixed onsite from separate $CO_2$ and $N_2$ sources. The use of custom gas blends brings new equipment into play, including gas blenders and possibly **nitrogen generators**.

## DEFINING MIXED GASES

For the purposes of this manual, as a convention in discussions involving mixed gas, the proportion of $CO_2$ will always be shown first, followed by the proportion of $N_2$.

### Blended Gas Bottles

Blended gas bottles are gas vendor-mixed $CO_2$ and $N_2$ gas mixes. Often called "G-Mix" or "Guinness Gas," these blends are typically available in blends of 25–30% $CO_2$ / 70–75% $N_2$ and are designed for use with nitrogenized or "nitro" beers. Although their use is commonplace, there are several limitations to this mixed gas source.

The physical characteristics of $CO_2$ limit the amount of blended gas that can be stored in a blended gas bottle compared to pure $CO_2$ or $N_2$. The tolerances of bottled blended gas are very difficult to manage during filling. Carbon dioxide becomes liquid at the very high pressures needed to compress $N_2$. Unless the bottled blend is well mixed, the bottle can become over-pressurized and the $CO_2$ can become a liquid. Because of this, blended gas bottles contain a very low volume of gas. It also means the blended gas being dispensed from the head space of the bottle will not be the blend proportion anticipated, resulting in over- or undercarbonated beer, increasing expense and decreasing draught beer quality. For these reasons, blended gas bottles are relatively expensive compared to other mixed gas sources such as gas blenders. When comparing the cost of a gas blender to the ongoing expense of premixed cylinder gas, the payback period for the blender is often under a year.

Another disadvantage of blended gas bottles is that the higher percentage of $CO_2$ that goes into the blend the lower the overall proportion that can go into the cylinder before the $CO_2$ becomes liquid. This limits most of the blends in premixed cylinders to very low $CO_2$ or "nitro" applications. If a high-percentage $CO_2$ blend is made available in a premixed cylinder the overall volume will be extremely low.

Premixed cylinders containing a mix of 25–30% $CO_2$ and 70–75% $N_2$ (i.e., G-Mix) are only intended for use with nitro beers. These blends are not intended for use with regularly carbonated beers (those with more than 2.0 volumes or 3.9 g/L of $CO_2$), even in high-pressure long-draw systems. Use of G-Mix gas on regularly carbonated beers causes these beers to lose carbonation in the keg or serving tank. After three to five days, the result is flat beer being served. This flat (undercarbonated) beer is more noticeable

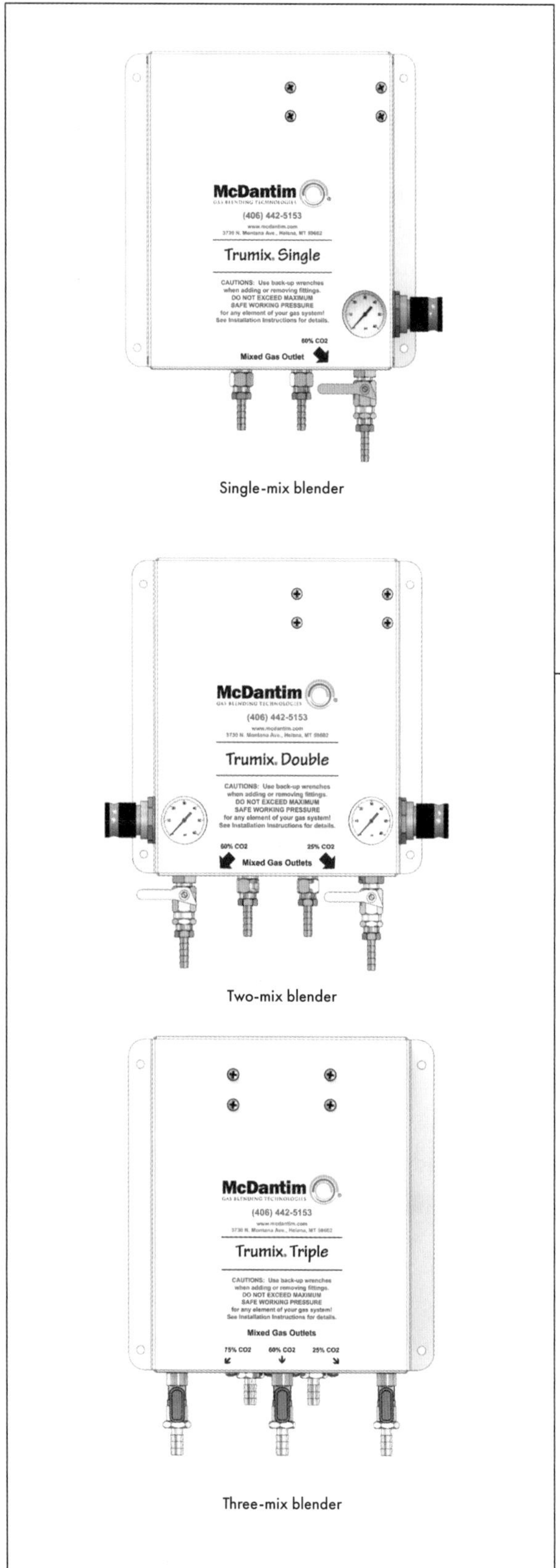


Single-mix blender

Two-mix blender

Three-mix blender

**Figure 4.11.** Gas blender options.

near the end of the keg, with the amount of flat beer increasing the longer the beer is in contact with this gas. Similarly, 100% $CO_2$ should not be used to dispense nitro beers, as they will overcarbonate very quickly and become unpourable.

## Gas Blenders

Gas blenders provide the most flexibility in obtaining mixed gas for dispensing beer. Gas blenders mix pure $CO_2$ and pure $N_2$ from individual tanks in specified ratios and can provide one, two, or even three blends on a single panel.

Single-mix blenders will typically contain a $CO_2$-rich blend designed for regularly carbonated beers. For simplicity, many installers would put in a blender with little thought or planning as to what the blend is, simply deferring to what was the commonly stocked 60%/40% blend. Recent studies in retail establishments have shown that a 70%/30% blend will more likely result in proper carbonation of draught beer in most retail draught systems. This has led the industry to stock the 70%/30% blend as the default blend for installers who do not specify a specific blend. This is not necessarily the best blend for every situation, however. The best approach for high-quality draught beer is to identify and use the exact correct gas blend for your particular draught system. See appendix C of this manual for examples of how to calculate this, or consult your professional draught beer equipment installer or supplier for more advice.

Two-mix blenders usually have one $CO_2$-rich blend for regularly carbonated beers and the second blend being a 25%/75% blend for nitro beers. Three-mix blenders will have two different $CO_2$-rich blends calculated to adequately serve beers with a reasonable range of $CO_2$ volumes (e.g., 2.2–2.8 volumes of $CO_2$), with the third blend being the 25%/75% blend for nitro beers. Existing one- and two-mix blenders can sometimes be upgraded to two- and three-mix blenders; be sure to check with your supplier. Recommended features for a gas blender include:

- an output mix that is preset by the manufacturer and is not adjustable onsite; and
- a blender that shuts down when either gas supply runs out, preventing damage due to running on only one gas.

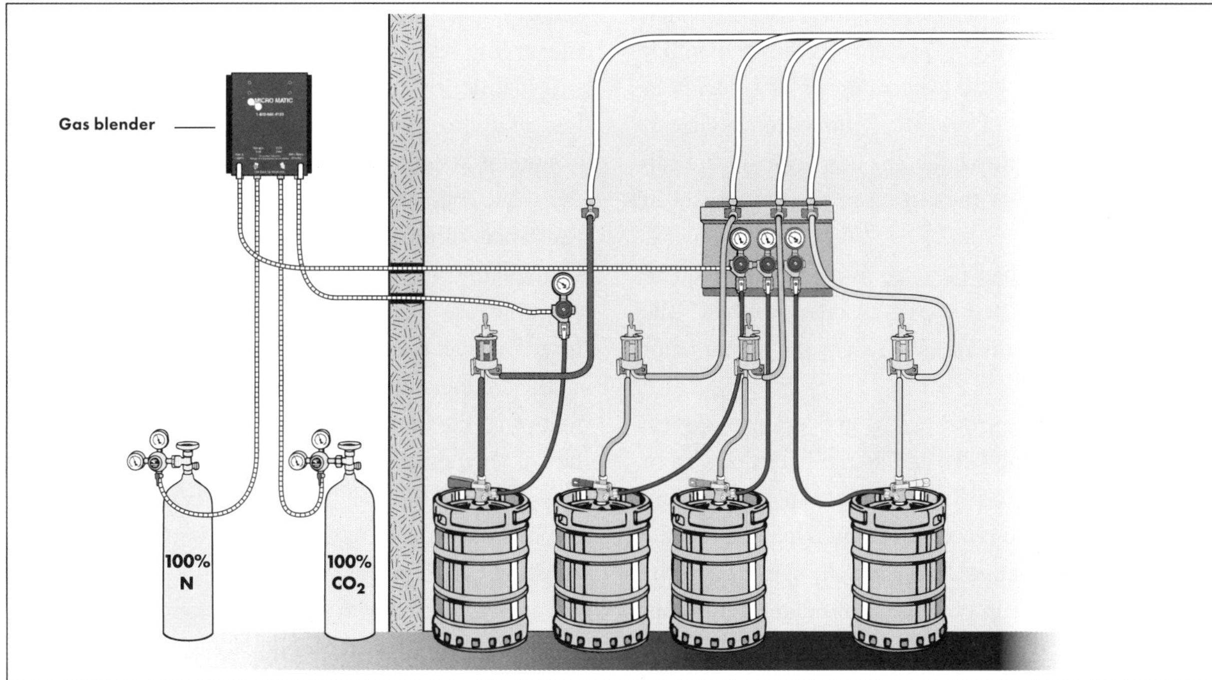


**Figure 4.12.** Typical setup for gas cylinders and gas blenders.

### Nitrogen Generators

Nitrogen generators extract $N_2$ from the atmosphere. Air is supplied by either a remote or integrated air compressor. Nitrogen generators are typically equipped with a built-in gas blender.

To protect $N_2$ purity from compromising draught beer quality, nitrogen generators should have the following features:

- $N_2$ production purity of at least 99.7%
- air inlets equipped with both an oil/water filter and a sterile air filter
- oil-free-type air compressors

All nitrogen generator filters should be inspected and replaced according to the manufacturer's specifications.

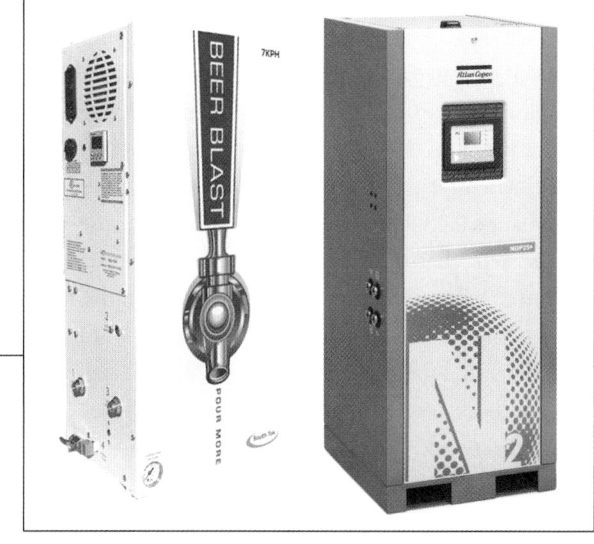


**Figure 4.13.** Two examples of nitrogen generators from South-Tek Systems, LLC (*left*) and Atlas Copco Compressors, LLC (*right*).

## SYSTEM BALANCE AND ACHIEVING FLOW

Having identified our type of dispensing gas, and then calculated our gas blend and applied pressure with the formulas in appendix C, we can now balance the elements of the long-draw draught system to achieve our desired flow rate. Our goal is to identify and add up all of the elements in the system that contribute to system resistance and get that figure to match the applied pressure in pounds per square inch.

### DRAUGHT SYSTEM BALANCE

When applied pressure equals system resistance, a draught system will pour clear-flowing beer at the rate of 1 gal./min., or approximately 2 fl. oz./sec.

In this manual we will be using degrees Fahrenheit (°F) for all temperature measurements. Just remember that *we want to know the temperature of the actual beer.* Since it takes a keg of beer many hours to stabilize at the temperature of the cooler, the beer temperature can vary quite a bit from the setting of the thermostat in your cooler.

We give the applied pressure in pounds per square inch, gauge abbreviated as psig, or often just "psi". The pressure applied to any keg is shown by the gas regulator attached to it.

Resistance comes from height and draught system components like the beer line as the beer flows from keg to faucet. We measure resistance in pounds (lb.) and account for two types, static and dynamic. For the purposes of this manual, and generally speaking in the trade, the resistance in pounds is considered equivalent to the pressure in pounds per square inch (psi) when balancing a draught beer system.

Static resistance comes from the effect of gravity, which opposes flow when beer is being pushed to a level above the keg. Here's one way to think about static resistance: if you have a U-shaped tube filled with water you can blow in one side and push the liquid up the other side of the tube. The weight of the liquid pushing back is the hydrostatic pressure. Each foot of increased elevation adds 0.43 lb. of hydrostatic pressure to a draught beer system that must be overcome by dispensing gas pressure. A figure of 0.5 lb./ft. is often used in the trade for ease of calculation, a convention that we will follow in this manual for purposes of discussion and example.

If the beer travels to a faucet above keg level, each foot of increased height will add approximately 0.5 lb. of resistance to the system. If the beer travels to a faucet below keg level, each foot of decreased elevation will subtract approximately 0.5 lb. of resistance from the system. When the keg and faucet heads are at the same height, static resistance is zero. This effect of gravity is independent of tube length, bends, junctions, or other configuration issues. In the past, the height difference used to determine static resistance was often measured from the base of the kegs being dispensed to the faucet height. Because a full keg will contain about 2½ ft. of beer, we recommend measuring from the middle of the keg being dispensed to the faucet height. Likewise, large serving vessels should be measured from the middle of the serving vessel fill height to the faucet height.

Dynamic resistance derives primarily from beer line, and also from some of the many components in a draught system (often called "hardware resistance"). Items like couplers and faucets usually impart negligible resistance, although some might have a specified value. Draught towers can range from zero to as high as 8 lb. of dynamic resistance; be sure to check with the manufacturer for exact tower resistance.

The combination of beer line tubing may include the following: the **jumper line**, which is typically five or six feet of vinyl or other flexible tubing that runs from the keg coupler to the wall bracket; the **trunk line**, which is the main section of tubing, usually barrier tubing, that runs the length of the system from the wall bracket in the cooler to the tower; and the **choker line**, which is a length of small-diameter tubing, usually 3⁄16" ID vinyl or other flexible tubing, that connects the trunk line to the stainless steel tubing or sometimes the back of the shank inside the tower. The choker is the biggest variable the installer uses to fine-tune system resistance to achieve balance. By varying the length of this high-resistance tubing, an installer can control flow rate to a large degree.

A few different specially designed devices can be used as alternatives to employing choker line restriction with 3⁄16" ID vinyl tubing. One such device consists of a series of plastic segments inserted into a short section of ¼" ID barrier tubing just below the tower. Another is a wire mesh device installed in the shank just behind the faucet. These devices are of varying restriction and, while potentially useful, also have some potential downsides. For one, these items prevent sponges being used for cleaning beer line. Additionally, the increased surface area may increase the likelihood of bacterial buildup or foaming.

These three components that contribute to dynamic resistance all have different resistance values. This is due to a combination of the tubing material, tubing diameter, and tubing length. Different resistance values in pounds per foot for commonly used materials and diameters are shown in table 4.1. (Note: Table 4.1 is provided as an example only. Please consult your equipment manufacturer for exact values for your specific beer line and system components.)

### TABLE 4.1. COMMON MATERIALS AND DIAMETERS USED FOR BEER LINE AND THEIR DYNAMIC RESISTANCE VALUES

| Type | Size | Resistance (lb./ft.)* | Volume (fl. oz./ft.) |
|---|---|---|---|
| Vinyl/flexible | 3/16" ID | 3.00 | 1/6 |
| Vinyl/flexible | 1/4" ID | 0.85 | 1/3 |
| Vinyl/flexible | 5/16" ID | 0.40 | 1/2 |
| Vinyl/flexible | 3/8" ID | 0.20 | 3/4 |
| Vinyl/flexible | 1/2" ID | 0.025 | 1 1/3 |
| Barrier | 1/4" ID | 0.30 | 1/3 |
| Barrier | 5/16" ID | 0.10 | 1/2 |
| Barrier | 3/8" ID | 0.06 | 3/4 |
| Stainless | 1/4" OD | 1.20 | 1/6 |
| Stainless | 5/16" OD | 0.30 | 1/3 |
| Stainless | 3/8" OD | 0.12 | 1/2 |

ID, internal diameter; OD, outside diameter.

*Restriction values may vary, depending on manufacturer.

Once the resistance values are obtained for the three main elements of dynamic resistance, plus any other significant parts (e.g., the tower), the total dynamic resistance is added to the static resistance for the system. This sum yields our **total system resistance.** When total system resistance (in pounds) is equal to the applied pressure (in psi) our flow rate will be one gallon per minute or 2 fl. oz./sec.

## DESIGNING FOR RESISTANCE

While the individual components in any draught system have a fixed resistance value, draught system designers can select from a variety of choices to hit the target total system resistance. For instance, a 20 ft. run of 1/4" ID vinyl beer line gives a total resistance of 17 psi, whereas 5/16" ID barrier tubing of the same length only generates 2 lb. of resistance. If the target resistance value is 20 psi, the 1/4" ID vinyl system would need one foot of 3/16" ID choker line added at the tower end to achieve the total system target resistance, whereas the 5/16" ID barrier tubing would need six feet of 3/16" ID choker line added at the tower end to reach the same target (see table 4.1). Whenever possible, systems should be designed so as to minimize, if not eliminate, the need for vinyl choker line at the tower end. The choker line is usually wrapped into a permanent installation where the recommended yearly change-out of vinyl tubing is not feasible.

Any draught system can be designed to operate under a range of applied pressure values. Whenever possible, the operating pressure will be set to maintain the proper carbonation level in the beer being served. Unfortunately, in some systems this is not possible. Consider the resistance created by long beer lines and climbs of two or more floors. Even using the lowest resistance components, the applied pressures for these systems often exceed that needed to maintain the appropriate beer carbonation level. Such systems must use mixed gas or pneumatic beer pumps to overcome the problem.

## ACCOMMODATING BEERS WITH VARYING CARBONATION

A common issue that arises with draught system design is how to deal with beers with varying levels of carbonation that are being dispensed on the same system. It is not uncommon to find a draught system stores all the beer at one temperature and pours them all with the same gas blend at the same operating pressure through draught lines that all have the same restriction value. The net result is that some beers may lose carbonation while other beers will gain carbonation within the same system. This one-size-fits-all setup is not ideal. In order to accommodate for differences in desired carbonation, we can make certain changes with the system equipment and setup parameters.

### $CO_2$ Percentage Adjustment

The adjustment of $CO_2$ percentages for different beers has historically been difficult, if not impossible. Gas blending panels usually have only one $CO_2$-rich blend available, with two-mix blenders typically accommodating nitrogenized beers with the second blend. Three-mix blenders are now available, which offer a nitro beer blend and two different $CO_2$-rich blends for regularly carbonated beers. As it turns out, most regularly carbonated beers can be divided into two general groups of carbonation level, 2.5 and 2.7 volumes $CO_2$ (see table 4.2). The higher percentage $CO_2$ blend can balance the higher carbonated beers. The new three-mix blender panels allow the installer to customize a gas blend for each of the two carbonation levels by following table 4.2.

**TABLE 4.2.** PERCENTAGE $CO_2$ FOR GAS BLENDS USED ON REGULARLY CARBONATED BEERS

| | Storage temp. | |
|---|---|---|
| | 35–37°F | 38–40°F |
| **Applied pressure** | **Median 2.5 volumes $CO_2$** | |
| 16–20 psi | 75–80% | 80–85% |
| 20–25 psi | 65% | 70% |
| **Applied pressure** | **Median 2.7 volumes $CO_2$** | |
| 16–20 psi | 80–85% | 80–90% |
| 20–25 psi | 70% | 75% |

### Applied Pressure Adjustment

Installers may choose to use a single gas blend for regularly carbonated beers and adjust the applied pressure on individual kegs to maintain proper carbonation. This is a helpful option in existing systems with a single $CO_2$-rich gas blend or when a multi-blend gas blender is not available for use. Regularly carbonated beers are divided into two different groups, 2.5 or 2.7 volumes $CO_2$, and the appropriate applied pressure for an individual beer can be determined according to table 4.3.

Most systems have all lines restricted equally, so applying different pressures to different beers will result in certain beers flowing faster or slower than others in the same system. These flow rate variances are normally not an issue and still allow for nearly optimal flow rates of around 2 fl. oz./sec., as long as the pressure variance between different beers is kept at or below 5 psi.

### Applied Pressure Adjustment with Flow-Control Faucets

In some instances, a beer's carbonation level can be so high that the limited pressure adjustment range alone still does not allow the beer to be poured. For these highly carbonated beers, the use of a flow-control faucet can be very helpful. A flow-control faucet has a restriction lever on the faucet itself, which allows the bartender to adjust the restriction of the system and the flow rate of the beer at the dispensing point. This allows the pressure to be significantly increased to keep a highly carbonated beer's carbonation level constant while still maintaining a manageable flow rate. Oftentimes the adjusted flow rate needs to be set much lower than 1 gal./min. (2 fl. oz./sec.), because even this standard flow rate can cause very highly carbonated beers to foam in the glass.

The use of flow-control faucets can be very helpful in all types of systems, including direct-draw systems using 100% $CO_2$. Some systems are outfitted with multiple gas blends inside the cooler and quick-disconnect fittings on individual gas lines. These setups allow the gas blend to a particular keg to be changed depending on the carbonation level and the pressure/gas blend combination needed to maintain the beer's proper carbonation.

**TABLE 4.3.** APPLIED PRESSURE SETTINGS FOR REGULARLY CARBONATED BEERS ACCORDING TO PERCENTAGE $CO_2$ IN GAS BLEND

| | | psi at 60% $CO_2$ | | | | psi at 65% $CO_2$ | | | | psi at 70% $CO_2$ | |
|---|---|---|---|---|---|---|---|---|---|---|---|
| | | 2.5 v/v | 2.7 v/v | | | 2.5 v/v | 2.7 v/v | | | 2.5 v/v | 2.7 v/v |
| **temp °F** | **40** | 27–33 | n/a | **temp °F** | **40** | 24–30 | 27–33 | **temp °F** | **40** | 21–26 | 24–29 |
| | **38** | 25–31 | 29–35 | | **38** | 22–28 | 26–31 | | **38** | 20–25 | 23–28 |
| | **37** | 25–30 | 28–34 | | **37** | 22–27 | 25–30 | | **37** | 19–24 | 22–27 |
| | **35** | 23–28 | 26–32 | | **35** | 20–25 | 23–28 | | **35** | 18–22 | 20–25 |

| | | psi at 75% $CO_2$ | | | | psi at 80% $CO_2$ | | | | psi at 85% $CO_2$ | |
|---|---|---|---|---|---|---|---|---|---|---|---|
| | | 2.5 v/v | 2.7 v/v | | | 2.5 v/v | 2.7 v/v | | | 2.5 v/v | 2.7 v/v |
| **temp °F** | **40** | 19–24 | 22–25 | **temp °F** | **40** | 17–21 | 19–24 | **temp °F** | **40** | 15–19 | 17–22 |
| | **38** | 17–22 | 20–25 | | **38** | 15–20 | 18–22 | | **38** | 14–18 | 16–20 |
| | **37** | 17–21 | 20–24 | | **37** | 15–19 | 17–21 | | **37** | 13–17 | 16–19 |
| | **35** | 16–20 | 18–22 | | **35** | 14–18 | 16–20 | | **35** | 12–16 | 14–18 |

**Notes:** v/v, volumes $CO_2$.
Add 1 psi for every 2000 ft. of elevation to account for differences in atmospheric pressure.

**Figure 4.14.** A Perlick flow-control faucet.

**Figure 4.15.** A flow-control faucet allows the bartender to maintain a manageable flow rate for highly carbonated beers.

## BALANCING DRAUGHT SYSTEMS

Having reviewed all the concepts behind draught system balance, it is instructive to compare two example systems to see how these variables are adjusted to create balanced draught systems in several different settings. The Example 1 (page 41) and Example 2 (page 42) callouts take you through the settings and calculations in each case example, using reference values from appendixes B and C.

## EXAMPLE 1: LONG-DRAW, CLOSED-REMOTE SYSTEM

This example for a long-draw, closed-remote system assumes that the dispensing gas blend mixture is already fixed; there is a vertical lift of 12 feet; and the beer trunk line total run is 120 feet. Find the operating pressure of the system, and then determine the appropriate tubing size for the trunks and choker-line tubing length.

**Beer Conditions**

Beer temperature: 35 °F
Beer carbonation: 2.6 volumes $CO_2$
Dispensing gas: 70% $CO_2$/30% $N_2$ blend

First, you must determine the gauge pressure of the blended gas required to maintain the correct level of carbonation. From Appendix C, this calculation is:

$$a = \left(\frac{b + 14.7}{c}\right) - 14.7$$

where *a* is the gauge pressure of the blended gas, *b* is the ideal gauge pressure of pure $CO_2$ for this situation (in this case, 10.7 psi; see table B.1 in appendix B), *c* is the proportion of $CO_2$ in the blended gas, and atmospheric pressure is assumed to be 14.7 psi (i.e., sea level).

$$a = \left(\frac{10.7 + 14.7}{0.70}\right) - 14.7$$
$$= (25.4/0.70) - 14.7$$
$$= 36.3 - 14.7$$
$$= 21.6 \text{ psi (round to 22 psi)}$$

**Static Resistance**

Vertical lift (faucet height above center of keg): 12 ft.

Static resistance = 12 ft. × 0.5 lb./ft.
= 6.0 lb.

**Balance**

The applied dispensing gas pressure of 22 psi must be balanced by the total system resistance. Since the static resistance equals 6 lb., the system will need a total of 16 lb. of dynamic resistance to be imparted by the beer line restriction.

Dynamic resistance = dispensing gas pressure – static resistance
= 22 – 6
= 16 lb.

**Beer Line Restriction**

120 ft. of 5/16" ID barrier tubing @ 0.1 lb./ft. (see table 4.1)
120 ft. × 0.1 lb./ft.= 12 lb.
1.3 ft. of 3/16" ID vinyl choker line @ 3.0 lb./ft.
1.3 ft. × 3.0 lb./ft. = 4 lb.
Dynamic resistance from barrier tubing and choker line:
12 + 4 = 16 lb.

## EXAMPLE 2: FORCED-AIR 10-FOOT RUN

In this example of a forced-air system, the beer cooler is directly over the bar. There is a 10 ft. fall from the center of the kegs to the faucet height, and the total run length is also exactly 10 ft.

**Beer Conditions**

Beer temperature: 33 °F
Beer carbonation: 2.8 volumes $CO_2$
Dispensing gas: 100% $CO_2$

We know the gauge pressure needed to maintain carbonation is 11.7 psig (see table B.1 in Appendix B).

**Static Resistance**

Vertical fall: 10 ft. (faucet is 10 ft. below the center of the keg)

Static resistance = 10 ft. × −0.5 lb./ft.
= −5.0 lb.

Note that the resistance here is negative. Because there is a drop between the keg and the faucet, the static resistance is contributing to the pressure applied by the gas to the beer.

**Balance**

The applied dispensing pressure of 11.7 psi combined with the 5 psi of static pressure (i.e., negative 5 lb. static resistance) must be balanced by the total system resistance. This balancing has to come from dynamic resistance imparted by the beer line restriction of 16.7 lbs.

Dynamic resistance required = 11.7 + 5
= 16.7 lb.

**Beer Line Restriction**

10 ft. of ¼" ID barrier tubing @ 0.3 lb./ft. (see table 4.1)
10 ft. × 0.3 lb./ft. = 3 lb.
4.6 ft. of 3⁄16" ID vinyl choker line @ 3 lb./ft.
4.6 ft. × 3 lb./ft. = 13.7 lb.
Dynamic resistance from barrier tubing and choker line:
3 + 13.7 = 16.8 lb. (close enough to our target of 16.7 lb.)

### NITROGENIZED (NITRO) BEERS

Nitrogenized, or nitro, beer is becoming more popular. It requires special attention, however, including a specific gas blend of $N_2$ and $CO_2$ as well as a unique faucet (see fig. 1.13 on page 13 for a detailed breakdown of a nitro faucet).

Nitrogenized beer was developed in the 1960s as a way to replicate the creaminess and low carbonation of cask conditioned ale. Normally, cask ales have carbonation levels that are significantly lower than force-carbonated beer and are pulled with a beer engine. Nitrogenization allowed retailers to be able to push a low-carbonated product to the dispensing faucet. Being able to push the low-carbonated beer instead of pulling it meant that brewers and retailers could, in effect, get close to a cask experience while having the benefits of modern draught dispensing systems.

**Figure 4.16.** Nitrogenized beer "cascades" when dispensed correctly.

**Figure 4.17.** Specially designed nitro faucets create turbulence to encourage nucleation of dissolved nitrogen gas upon dispense.

What is nitrogenized beer? First, it is important to note that $N_2$ does not easily dissolve in beer because its stable, non-polar molecular structure makes it much less soluble in aqueous solution than, say, $CO_2$. This means $N_2$ does not dissolve at lower pressures—the kind of pressures encountered in long-draw dispensing systems—making it is the perfect medium to apply the "push" necessary to get the beer where it needs to go without changing the properties of the beer. Second, it is possible to force $N_2$ into solution in beer, but this is

Photo © Getty/Camrocker (nitrogenized beer), Getty/Instants

done at pressures far exceeding dispensing pressure and is done at the brewery. And third, $N_2$ in a nitro beer is only there to augment the existing $CO_2$, which typically ranges from 1.1 to 1.7 volumes. The amount of $N_2$ actually forced into the beer is so small that it is measured in parts per million and not volumes.

Solubility of $CO_2$ is affected much more by temperature than is the solubility of $N_2$. The takeaway is that a nitrogenized beer is still a carbonated beer (albeit at much lower volumes $CO_2$ than a typical beer) that also contains a small amount of $N_2$.

Since nitrogenized beer has had a small amount of $N_2$ coerced into it at high pressure, it must maintain a relatively high applied pressure to keep the $N_2$, and the $CO_2$ in solution (for each gas dissolved in a solution, there is a relationship between the gas's concentration and partial pressure). And, since the amount of $CO_2$ is far below that of a regular beer, the applied pressure ratio of $N_2$ to $CO_2$ will be much greater. The volumes of $CO_2$ in the beer and the applied pressure calculation will work off of the same solubility charts that are used for the other dispensing calculations. Unfortunately, most charts do not go below 2.0 volumes of $CO_2$ and most nitrogenized beer is around 1.2 volumes. Because of this, we recommend the use of online calculators, such as the McDantim EasyBlend Calculator shown in figure 4.18.

The typical gas blend for nitrogenized beers at 1.2 volumes of $CO_2$ is 25% $CO_2$ / 75% $N_2$ (this keeps the $CO_2$ in solution at the required carbonation). Using the McDantim EasyBlend Calculator, the proper pressure for a nitrogenized 5.5% ABV (alcohol affects solubility) beer carbonated to 1.2 volumes $CO_2$ that is dispensed at 38°F in Denver (5280 ft. above sea level) with a blend of 25% $CO_2$ will be 37.8 psi (fig. 4.18). As the individual parameters of a given beer change, so will the applied pressure.

This special 25%/75% high-pressure gas blend keeps the two gases in solution as the brewer intended. Non-nitrogenized beers should not be poured on such a blend. The $CO_2$ in regularly carbonated beers will equalize over time to the $CO_2$ volumes of the nitrogenized beer (usually 1.1–1.7) but without the benefit of having had $N_2$ already dissolved in the beer. Applied pressure with a psi in the mid-30s is not enough to force $N_2$ into the beer. It WILL go flat and there will be no creamy head.

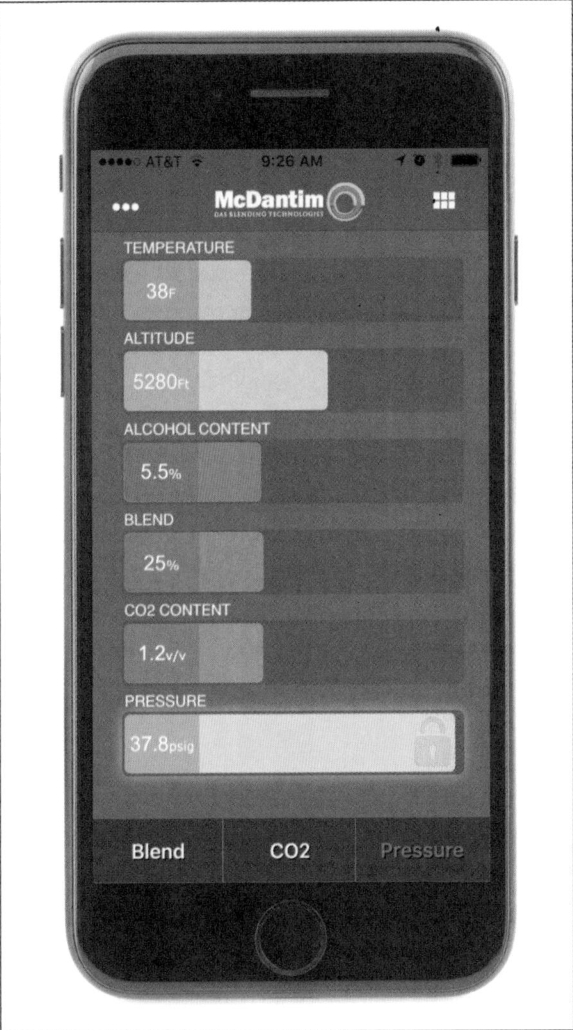


**Figure 4.18.** A screenshot of the McDantim EasyBlend Calculator app, which can be a useful tool for balancing draught systems.

The high pressure required by a nitrogenized beer must be balanced within the system, which is done with a unique nitrogen, or nitro, faucet. These faucets apply additional resistance in the form of a restriction plate found within the housing of the faucet. It forces the beer through five tiny holes (of varying diameter, which will add or detract resistance) and typically account for around 20 lb. of added resistance to the system.

In addition, the restrictor plate of a nitro faucet has the added function of helping to break the $N_2$ out of the beer, that is, the $N_2$ comes out of solution back into the gas phase. Nitrogen, though difficult to get into the beer, needs coaxing to come back out (because the atmosphere is 78% $N_2$ gas, $N_2$ in solution does not readily want to leave). The agitation due to the beer being forced through the tiny holes, combined with the sudden drop in pressure, will do the trick. The pressure in psi on one side of the plate is in the mid-30s while the other side is somewhere around 14.7 psi, if at sea level (this will vary depending on the altitude of the premises). This pressure drop causes both the $N_2$ and $CO_2$ to break out. These two gases move from the dissolved phase to the gaseous phase at different rates. The small $N_2$ bubbles that form begin to move to the surface of the liquid in a slower fashion than the $CO_2$ bubbles. It is the breakout of the slower $N_2$ and the faster $CO_2$ together that causes the cascading effect so interesting in the presentation of a nitro beer. The $N_2$ bubbles create a creamy head, which stays around for a longer period of time because of the high concentration of $N_2$ in the air. In other words, the $N_2$ gas in the head has nowhere in particular to go, so the bubbles tend not to coalescence (i.e., they don't get bigger and pop).

The distance of the draw is typically not a factor for nitro beers because an applied pressure in psi in the mid-30s is enough to push the beer to the faucet in almost all long-draw systems (pouring without an added pump). And, the restrictor plate will ensure an even, consistent flow from the faucet.

The importance of using a specialized faucet and a specific gas blend with nitrogenized beer cannot be overstated. Nitrogenized beer will not pour correctly if treated as a regularly carbonated beer. At the same time, trying to pour regularly carbonated beer under conditions designed for a nitro beer will also be problematic.

## COOLING

As with many direct-draw systems, the kegs in a long-draw system reside in a walk-in cooler held at 34–38°F. But for long-draw systems additional cooling components that surround the beer lines themselves are used to keep beer cold throughout its journey from keg to faucet. We find two common designs, air-cooled and glycol-cooled.

In a **forced-air long-draw system**, beer lines travel through a tube or chase kept cold by a continuously operating recirculation fan. The fan pushes cold air from a condensing unit inside the cooler into and through the ductwork. In both single-duct and double-duct systems, cold air travels a route from the cooler to and through the tap tower as well as a return route back to the cooler. Single-duct systems use a tube-in-tube design effective for runs of up to 15 ft. Runs of up to 25 ft. can be created using double-duct systems where separate tubes carry the outbound and return flows. These forced-air systems can be especially vulnerable to temperature fluctuations in the outside environment. All ductwork should be well insulated. Temperatures around the room should be carefully assessed before installation. It is important to note that temperatures near the ceiling of an already hot basement or storage room where the ducts may run can be significantly higher than at ground level.

It is also important to consider the extra cooling load placed on the keg cooler with such an

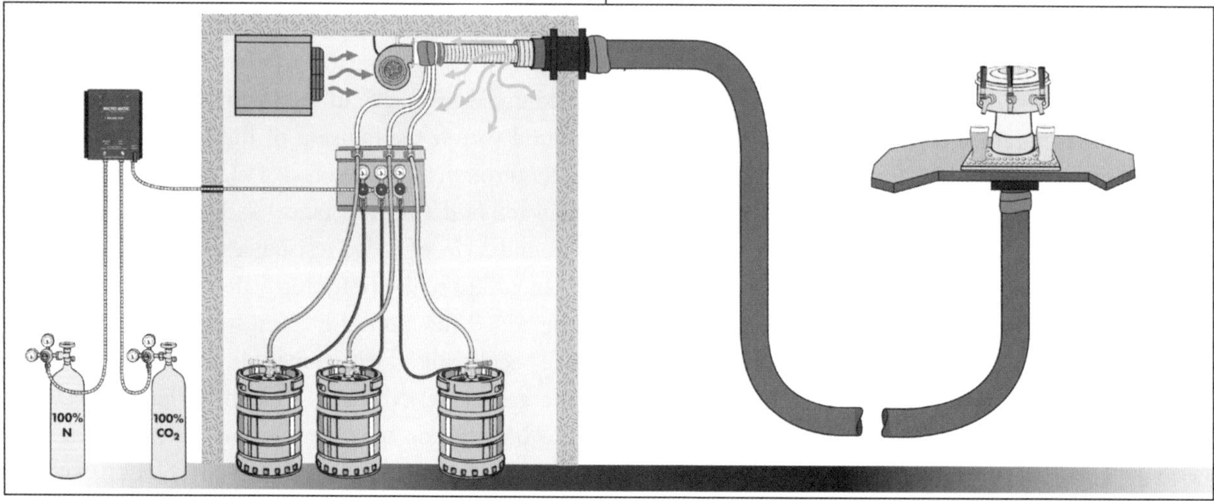


**Figure 4.19.** Single-duct air-cooled system.

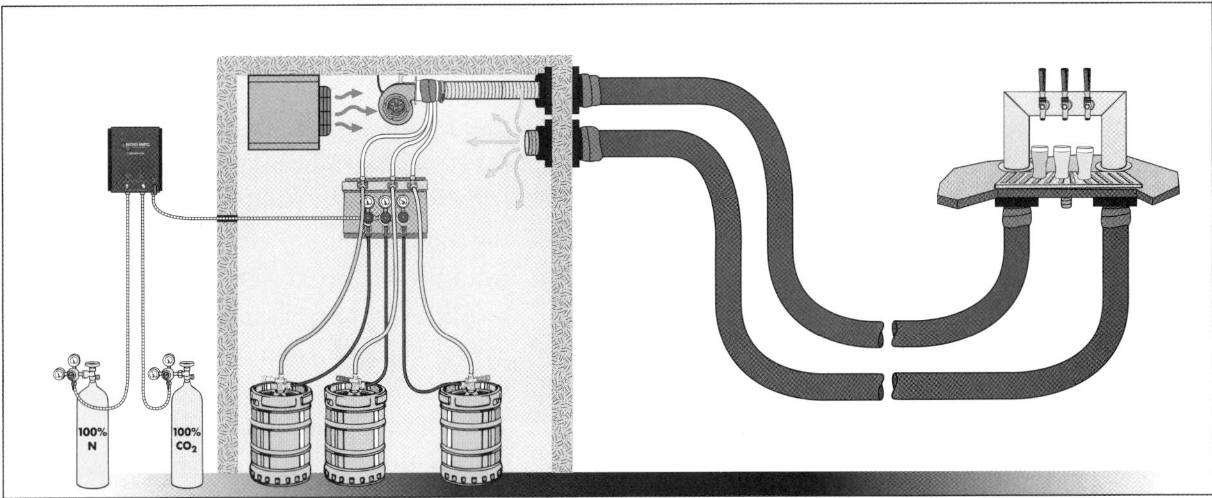


**Figure 4.20.** Double-duct air-cooled system.

**Figure 4.21.** Glycol chiller.

installation. Many coolers are specifically designed to cool the exact dimensions of the walk-in cooler, and adding a forced-air system may overload and compromise the entire cooling system.

Glycol-cooled long-draw systems service runs longer than 25 feet. Here, a separate chiller (fig. 4.21) pumps a chilled mixture of water and food-grade liquid **propylene glycol** through cooling lines parallel to and in contact with the beer lines. These systems require well-insulated and carefully configured trunk line. Each beer line (usually barrier line) in a trunk touches a glycol line to keep the beer cold as it travels from keg to faucet (fig. 4.22). Glycol chillers work well as long as they are maintained properly; see suggested maintenance points in the following section.

Glycol towers attach coolant lines parallel to the beer lines (typically stainless steel tubing) and surround them tightly with insulation. This cooling method allows towers to be located remotely from the cold box, up to several hundred feet away.

In addition to the glycol chiller used to maintain cold temperatures in the beer lines, some systems, like those using frosted or "ice" towers, use a separate glycol cooling system to chill the faucet tower.

### Glycol Chiller Maintenance

Glycol chillers are key components to long-draw dispensing systems. Glycol chillers are much less expensive to maintain than they are to replace; regular maintenance will increase both their service life and dependability. The list that follows describes some recommended maintenance practices; be sure to check with your manufacturer for items and procedures specific to your chillers.

- *Glycol bath:* Keep the cover of the glycol bath closed to prevent water vapor from diluting the strength of the glycol.

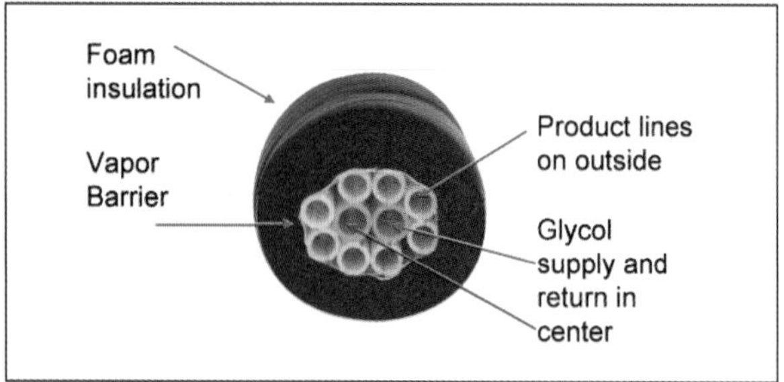


**Figure 4.22.** Photograph showing a cross-section of a typical draught line bundle with glycol lines.

- *Glycol bath temperature:* Check the temperature of the glycol bath every two weeks, making sure it is within the range specified by the manufacturer. Many chillers have temperature gauges that are easily visible from the outside.
- *Motors:* Check motors monthly to confirm smooth-sounding operation; look for signs of overheating.
- *Pumps:* Check pumps monthly for smooth-sounding operation; check connections and insulation for leaks or missing insulation.
- *Condenser:* Inspect the condenser monthly for dirt and airflow obstructions and clean as necessary. Remove and clean grills to expose the condenser fins. Remove all contaminants from the fin surface by using a stiff bristle brush, vacuum cleaner, or compressed gas discharged from the fan side of the condenser.
- *Trunk line:* Visually inspect trunk lines every six months for signs of ice buildup, insulation damage, and glycol leakage.
- *Glycol mixture:* Check viscosity and condition of glycol-water cooling mixture every six months. Test freezing point every 18 months with a refractometer and adjust or replace glycol mixture as needed. Typical ranges are 20–25% glycol; be sure the glycol concentration follows manufacturer recommendations. ■

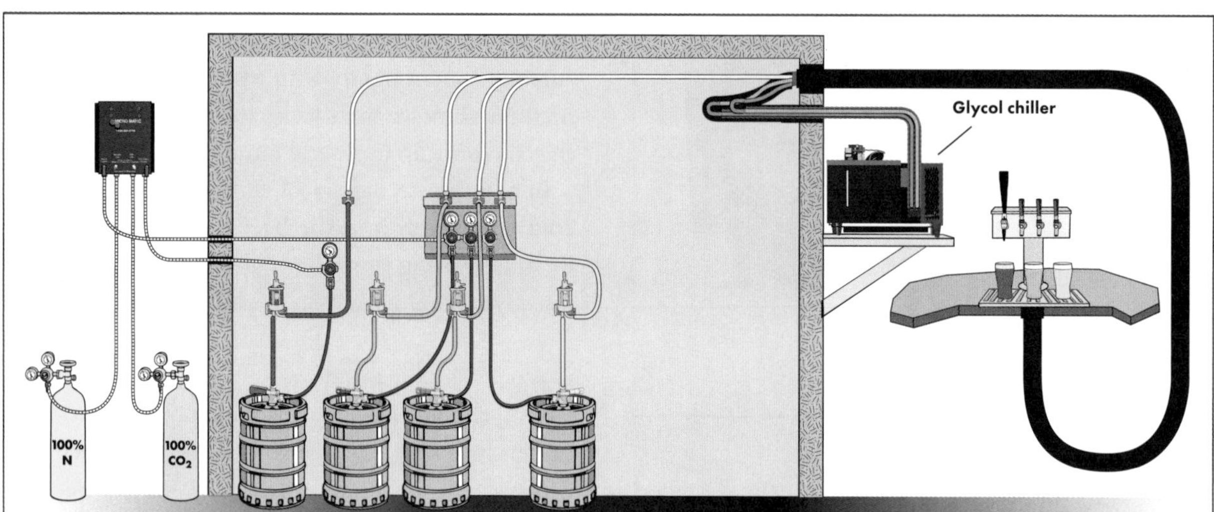


**Figure 4.23.** Glycol chiller in long-draw system.

# Section II

# DRAUGHT SYSTEM OPERATIONS

Draught systems from simple to complex can deliver high-quality beer—but only when properly operated and suitably maintained. Many who work with draught beer will never have the chance to buy or install the system components discussed in **section I**, but all will pour beer from the faucet and nearly everyone will experience foaming or other problems at some time that can be traced to operating conditions. In **section II** of this manual, we consider all the issues involved in operating a draught system and serving the customer a top-quality draught beer.

**Chapter 5** covers practical issues related to the cooler and other "behind the scenes" aspects of beer service. **Chapter 6** looks at glass cleaning and the proper way to pour a beer.

**Chapter 7** concludes our discussion of operating issues by taking a close look at maintenance and cleaning. Whether you clean your system yourself or hire an outside service, you owe it to yourself to understand proper cleaning methods. Without this knowledge, you cannot defend against a decline in beer quality at your establishment. Finally, **chapter 8** looks at steps that anyone can follow to troubleshoot issues and solve draught beer dispensing problems. ■

5

# PREPARATION TO POUR

While many of the issues relating to draught beer quality concern system settings and activities that occur at the bar, some operating issues require attention behind the scenes as well. In this chapter, we will present a checklist of system settings that will assist you in delivering great draught beer to the consumer, including a keg temperature guide as well as other behind-the-scenes preparations that will affect draught system performance. Finally, we will cover some guidelines for linking kegs in series.

## BEHIND THE SCENES CHECKLIST

Before you can be sure your draught system will operate properly and consumers are served the best possible beer, we recommend attention to the following items.

### Outside the Cooler

1. Install a $CO_2$ detector where necessary; check any confined-space $CO_2$ detector for the area where you are working in order to stay safe and stay alive.
2. Check the glycol bath operating temperature is in the 29–32°F range.
3. Visually check the dispensing gas cylinders; a full $CO_2$ cylinder = 800 psi; a full $N_2$ cylinder = 2200 psi. Bulk $CO_2$ tank gauges operate on an "E" for empty and "F" for full scale. Nitrogen generators operate on a pressurized gauge (set to above 100 psi, check manufacturer's instructions).
4. Check the beer line cleaning log. Beer lines should be cleaned every 7–14 days (check local ordinances for your area concerning the required frequency.)

Inside the Cooler

1. Air temperature inside the cooler should be 36–38°F.
2. Liquid temperature thermometer should read 36–38°F.
3. Draught beer lines should be full of beer and free of bubbles or kinks.
4. Draught beer on tap is within the brewer's freshness window for dispensing (varies by brewer). Beer flavor in kegs that have been on tap for longer than 45 days may have changed compared to the intended flavor.
5. Check the cooler is free of beer leaks, drips, or spills.
6. Check that all FOBs in the system are in the pouring position.
7. Check that all FOB drains are empty and free of buildup.
8. Visually check all gas pressure gauges are operating at the ideal pressure setting:
   a. Direct-draw system using 100% $CO_2$ for ales and lagers = 12–15 psi
   b. Long-draw system using blended 60–80% $CO_2$ (rich blend) for ales and lagers = 22–25 psi
   c. Premixed 25% $CO_2$/75% $N_2$ blend (for nitrogenized beers only) with restrictor faucet = 30–35 psi
   d. For precise settings, refer to the McDantim app (Figure 4.18) discussed in chapter 4.
9. Visually check that gas valves are in the open position.
10. Listen and feel around gas connections for leaks; large leaks will make an audible hiss.
11. Ensure all food products are stored away from kegs and beer lines. Dedicated beer coolers are recommended.

At the Tower

1. Flush the faucets with clean water and wipe dry with a clean microfiber towel.
2. Pour 1–3 fl. oz. of beer to make sure the faucet works properly. Evaluate what you pour to confirm the tap marker matches the beer in the line.
3. Wipe down surfaces so that they are free of beer spills.
4. Check for fruit flies and other bugs living around the draught tower.
5. Check that glassware is free of any aromas, dust, lipstick, and other imperfections.

These routine checks will keep you and your staff in control of the operating conditions of your draught system. They will help you be proactive and prevent disruptions to service and delivery in your draught beer system.

## COLD STORAGE AND PROPER CHILLING OF KEGS BEFORE SERVING

To ensure fresh flavor and easy dispensing, draught beer should remain at or slightly below 38°F throughout distribution, warehousing, and delivery. Brewers and distributors use refrigerated storage for draught beer. In warm climates or long routes, they may also use insulating blankets or refrigerated delivery trucks to minimize temperature increases during shipping.

At retail, increases of even a few degrees above 38°F can create pouring problems, especially excessive foaming. Ideally, all draught beer delivered to retail will be stored cold until served.

### DRAUGHT SAFETY

Buddy-lifting or use of a mechanical lifting system is recommended when moving kegs. A keg will typically weigh 165 lb. when full. Be aware of pinch-points and never get below a rolling or sliding keg.

Accounts that lack cold storage for their entire inventory of draught beer should allow adequate chilling time for recently refrigerated kegs in order to avoid problems when dispensing. In a similar vein, recently arrived kegs should be allowed adequate chilling time as the contents usually warm up to some degree during delivery. In order to avoid dispensing problems, every keg must be at or below 38°F when being served. To help ensure that your kegs are properly chilled before serving, table 5.1 provides a guide to the approximate time needed to properly chill a keg to 38°F from a given starting temperature. Note that even kegs that "feel cold" (e.g., 44°F) may need to chill overnight in order to ensure proper dispensing. Table 5.2 shows how quickly a keg will warm up when exposed to temperatures above 38°F. From table 5.2, it is clear that a keg will warm up from 38°F to 44°F during delivery or storage at ambient temperature after only four or five hours. But, looking back at table 5.1, we see that same keg will need to be in the cooler for a full 18 hours before reaching a proper serving temperature of 38°F again.

**TABLE 5.1.** TIME REQUIRED TO CHILL A KEG TO 38°F FROM VARIOUS TEMPERATURES

| Starting temp. | Hours to reach 38°F |
|---|---|
| 50°F | 25.0 |
| 48°F | 23.5 |
| 46°F | 21.0 |
| 44°F | 18.0 |
| 40°F | 7.0 |
| 38°F | 0 |

**TABLE 5.2.** INCREASE IN KEG TEMPERATURE OVER TIME FROM A 38°F STARTING TEMPERATURE

| Time (hours) | Temp |
|---|---|
| 0 | 38°F |
| 1 | 39°F |
| 2 | 41°F |
| 3 | 42°F |
| 4 | 43°F |
| 5 | 45°F |
| 6 | 48°F |

### LINKING KEGS IN SERIES

Busy accounts may connect kegs in a series or in a chain to meet peak demand. Chaining two or three kegs of the same product together allows all of the chained kegs to be emptied before beer stops flowing. The first keg in the series will be tapped with a normal coupler. The second (and subsequent) kegs in the series require that the check valve be removed from the gas side of the coupler (see figures 1.8 and 1.9 in chapter 1). Tap the first keg with the normal coupler. Instead of sending the beer line from this first coupler to the bar faucet, connect it to the $CO_2$ inlet on the second keg's coupler. Subsequent kegs can be attached the same way. When pressurized and pouring, beer flows from the first keg to the second and on to the third before it travels to the faucet. Once set, this arrangement will dispense the contents of all the chained kegs before it runs empty. A series arrangement should only be used in accounts that will "turn" or empty kegs rapidly. The

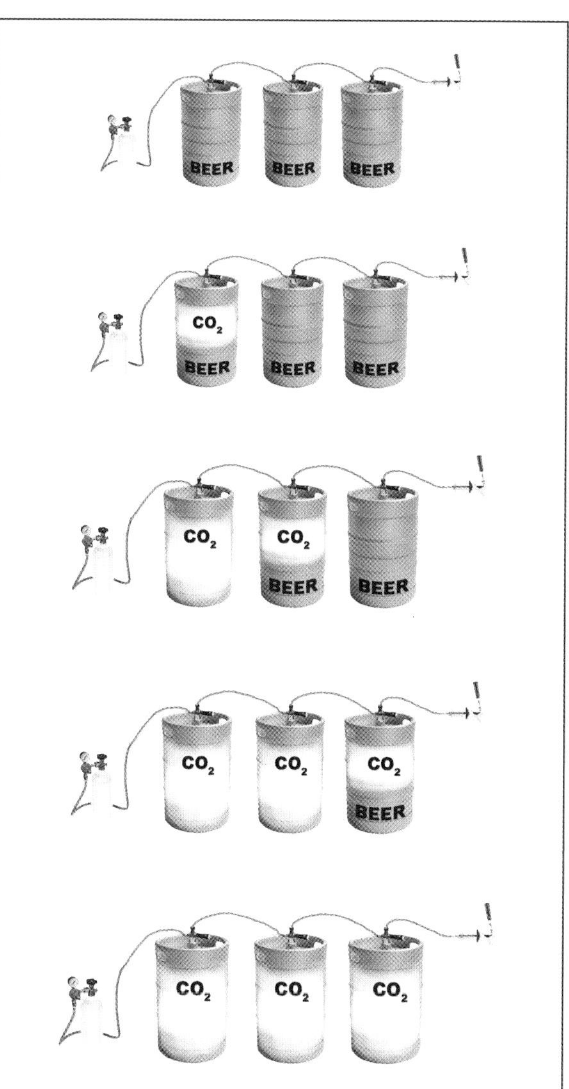


**Figure 5.1.** Kegs linked in a series should be chained so that the keg closest to the faucet empties last.

account needs to completely empty the entire series on a regular basis (every seven days is a common best practice at breweries). Failure to empty the series completely leaves old beer in the system. If a fresh keg is being rotated into a system that is not run completely dry, it is important to tap it in front of any empty or partial kegs in the system. *This prevents foaming from beer entering a keg that is not already full.* Figure 5.1 illustrates the progressive emptying of chained kegs. ■

# 6

# SERVING DRAUGHT BEER

Properly designed and appropriately operated, your draught system will dispense perfect draught beer from its faucets. But the consumer's experience can still be ruined by improper pouring, residue in glassware, and unsanitary practices. In this chapter, we review the serving practices required to deliver high quality draught beer.

To achieve the consumer experience the brewer intended, beer must be served following specific conditions and techniques. Let's review some of the conditions critical to proper draught dispense.

- Beer should be stored between 34°F and 38°F.
- Beer should be served between 38°F and 44°F.
- To accomplish proper temperature control, the glycol lines that cool the beer lines in a long-draw system should be set between 29°F and 32°F.
- The draught system should be balanced (pressure = resistance).
- The normal flow rate should be 2 fl. oz./sec.

## GLASSWARE CLEANING

A perfectly poured beer requires a properly cleaned glass. As a starting point, glassware must be free of visible soil and marks. A beer-clean glass is also free of foam-killing residues and lingering aromatics such as **sanitizer**.

A freshly cleaned glass should be used for every pour. We recommend that retailers never refill a used glass, a practice that may also violate local health codes.

Two systems deliver effective beer glass cleaning: manual cleaning in a three-tub sink, and dedicated automatic glass washers. Each approach requires specific techniques and a certain degree of discipline. Let's look at what's involved with each one.

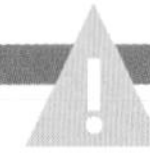

## DRAUGHT SAFETY

Glassware sanitizing is accomplished with chlorine or quaternary ammonium compounds (also called quats). Know the correct dilution for your sink volume—excess sanitizer does not do a better job than the correct concentration and may be unhealthy for staff and customers. Keep chlorine levels at 100 ppm and quat levels at 200 ppm unless your local authority requires otherwise. Keep safety data sheets (SDSs) nearby for reference. Regularly review sanitizer procedures with staff.

### Manual or Hand Cleaning in a Three-Tub Sink

1. Clean sinks and work area prior to starting in order to remove any chemicals, oils, or grease from other cleaning activities or detergents.
2. Empty residual liquid from the dirty glass to a drain. Glasses should NOT be emptied into the cleaning water as it will dilute the cleaning solutions.
3. In the first tub, clean the glass in hot water and suitable detergent. Detergent must not be fat- or oil-based. Detergents suitable for beer glass cleaning are available through restaurant and bar suppliers.
4. Scrub the glass with cleaning brushes to remove film, lipstick, and other residue. Rotate the glass on the brushes to scrub all interior and exterior surfaces. Be sure to clean the inside bottom of the glass.
5. In the second tub, rinse the glass heel to toe in cold water. Water for the rinse should not be stagnant but should be continually refreshed via an overflow tube. If time permits, a double dunk is recommended and preferred.
6. Sanitize the rinsed glass in a third tub filled with water and an appropriate sanitizer. Consult the sanitizer manufacturer's instructions regarding appropriate water temperature. Sanitizers typically contain chlorine, so check the pH and chlorine content of the sanitizing bath periodically to maintain proper conditions. Chlorine concentration should be 100 ppm or at the required local health department concentration.

**Figure 6.1.** Typical three-tub sink setup.

**Figure 6.2.** *Left:* In the three-tub sink system, residual beer must be poured to a drain, not the cleaning water. *Right:* Glasses are rinsed in the second tub between detergent and sanitizer tubs.

### Automatic Glass-Washing Machines

1. Dedicate this machine to cleaning bar and beer glassware only. Do not subject it to food or dairy product residue.
2. Use the correct detergent, sanitizer, and rinse agents in properly metered amounts.
3. Check detergent, sanitizer, and rinse agent concentrations once each day using kits, or follow the chemical supplier's recommendations.
4. Use water temperatures of 130°F to 140°F. High-temperature machines designed to operate at 180°F can be used without additional chemical sanitizers. Please check your health department for local requirements.
5. Maintain the machine to assure good water flow through the system, including free flow through each nozzle and washer arm. Drain and refill the machine multiple times each day to ensure fresh rinse water is available after peak service times.
6. Regularly service the machine based on the manufacturer's or installer's guidelines.

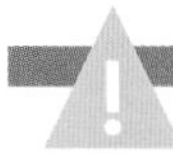

## DRAUGHT SAFETY

Low-foam glassware detergents can be caustic. Use care when dispensing detergents to avoid skin or eye contact. Personal protective equipment (PPE) is recommended. Clean up spills or skin contact immediately with large volumes of water. Keep the detergent SDS nearby and regularly review safety procedures with staff. Consult the SDS or chemical supplier for proper use.

### Handling Clean Glasses

To keep glassware clean and odor-free after washing:

1. Air-dry the clean glassware. Drying glasses with a towel can leave lint and may transmit germs and odors.
2. Dry and store glasses in a stainless-steel wire basket to provide maximum air circulation. Similar deeply corrugated baskets or surfaces also work.
3. Do not dry or store glassware on a towel, rubber drain pad, or other smooth surface, as they can transfer odors to the glass and slow the drying process.
4. Store glassware in an area free of odors, smoke, grease, and dust.
5. Store beer glasses dry in a chiller. Never use a freezer. Chill glasses at 36–40°F.
6. Store chilled glasses in a separate refrigerator away from food products, such as meat, fish, cheese, or onions, as they can impart an odor to the glasses.

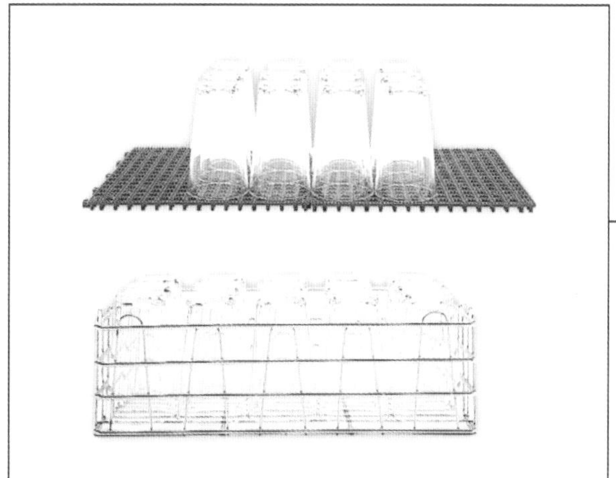

**Figure 6.3.** Clean glasses should be allowed to air dry.

### TESTING FOR "BEER-CLEAN" GLASS

Beer poured to a beer-clean glass forms a proper head and creates residual lacing as the beer is consumed. After cleaning, you can test your glasses for beer-clean status using three different techniques: sheeting, the salt test, and lacing. Let's review each technique.

***Sheeting test.*** For the sheeting test, dip the glass in water. If the glass is clean, water evenly coats the glass when lifted out of the water. If the glass still has an invisible film, water will break up into droplets on the inside surface.

***Salt test.*** In the salt test, salt sprinkled on the interior of a wet glass will adhere evenly to the clean surface, but will not adhere to the parts that still contain a greasy film. Poorly cleaned glasses show an uneven distribution of salt.

***Lacing test.*** For the lacing test, fill the glass with beer. If the glass is clean, foam will adhere to the inside of the glass in parallel rings after each sip, forming a lacing pattern. If not properly cleaned, foam will adhere in a random pattern, or may not adhere at all.

**Figure 6.4.** Three properly cleaned glasses used to show the three methods for testing beer-clean glassware.

## GLASSWARE TEMPERATURE

Part of dispensing draught beer at the correct temperature for the consumer involves paying attention to the temperature of glassware during service.

- Serving between 38°F and 44°F delivers the best taste experience for most beer styles. Domestic lager beer can be enjoyed at 38°F to 40°F if served in a chilled glass. Beer served at near-frozen temperatures retains more $CO_2$ gas (resulting in a more filling experience for the consumer) and blinds the taste experience (taste buds are numbed, resulting in a bland taste experience) in comparison with beer served at recommended temperatures.
- Room-temperature glasses are preferred for craft beer but may cause foaming with highly carbonated beer.
- Chilled glasses are preferred for domestic lager beer, but they should be DRY before chilling. Wet glassware should not be placed in a freezer or cooler as it may create a sheet of ice inside the glass.
- Frozen glasses will create foaming due to a sheet of ice being formed when the beer is introduced to the glass. Extremely cold glass surfaces will cause beer to foam due to a rapid release of $CO_2$ from the product.
- Water mist devices may be used to pre-wet and chill the glass interior prior to filling. Glass interior should be mostly free of excess water before pouring. Water supplied to the mist device should be filtered and free of aromas such as chlorine.

## POURING DRAUGHT BEER

Proper serving of draught beer is intended to result in a "controlled" release of carbonation to give a better sensory experience. The evolution of $CO_2$ gas during pouring builds the foam head and releases desirable flavors and aromas.

**Figure 6.5.** Properly pouring draught beer is a four-step process.

### Technique

As illustrated in figure 6.5, properly pouring draught beer is a four-step process:

1. Hold the glass at a 45° angle, open faucet fully (fig. 6.5, *top left*).
2. Gradually tilt the glass upright once beer has reached about the halfway point in the glass (fig. 6.5, *bottom left*).
3. Pour beer straight down into the glass, working the glass to form a one-inch collar of foam (the head). This is for visual appeal as well as carbonation release (fig. 6.5, *bottom left*).
4. Close the faucet quickly to avoid wasteful overflow (fig. 6.5, *bottom right*).

While retailers struggle with customers who demand their beer "filled to the rim," brewers prefer beer poured with about a one-inch collar of foam, which is the beer's "head" (fig. 6.6). The importance of a one-inch foam collar should not be underestimated. A one-inch head maximizes retailer profit, as foam is 25% to 33% beer. Filling a glass to the rim is overpouring. Moreover, a proper head on a draught beer delivers the total sensory experience, including the following sensory benefits:

- a good pour has visual appeal
- the beer releases more aromatic volatiles
- the palate-cleansing effects of carbonation are enhanced
- the beer presents better overall textural and sensorial qualities to the consumer

**Figure 6.6.** Brewers intend their beers to be perfectly carbonated when poured, resulting in a one-inch foam collar *(left)*. Undercarbonation *(middle)* and overcarbonation *(right)* result in wastage and an inferior sensory experience.

### Pouring Hygiene

Proper hygienic technique should always be observed when pouring draught beer.

- In no instance should a faucet nozzle touch the inside of the glass.
  - Nozzles can cause glassware to break; nozzles can also transfer contamination from dried beer to glassware.
- In no instance should the faucet nozzle become immersed in the consumer's beer.
  - Nozzles dipped in beer become a breeding ground for microorganisms.

### Free-Flow Pouring

Beer pours best from a fully open faucet. To control the faucet during operation, hold the handle firmly at the base. Partially open faucets cause inefficiency and poor quality, namely:

- turbulent flow,
- excessive foaming,
- wasted beer.

### Faucet Hygiene

We recommend quickly rinsing faucets and drip trays with fresh water at the close of business each day and allowing the faucet to air dry. Studies have indicated that, in retail locations that use this simple step, the faucets and beer lines stay significantly cleaner and fruit flies are not as evident around faucets and drip trays. As an added benefit, the faucet won't become sticky as beer dries out, so the first pour the next day will be much easier since the handle will move readily.

For notes on proper dispensing hygiene when using a cask ale beer engine, see appendix D.

## GROWLERS

Growlers are a great way to bring draught beer with you. The practice of bringing draught beer home started in the late 1800s. Patrons would bring a galvanized pail to their local watering hole and have it filled with beer. A lid was placed on the pail and the sound of the escaping carbonation was said to "growl."

Today we have many clean and hygienic ways of transporting draught beer, including glass, ceramic, stainless steel, and aluminum. The lids can be flip-top or screw-on. The size can vary from 32 to 64 fl. oz. It is important to make sure that the vessel you choose is pressure rated and designed to be used for carbonated liquid. The lid is important also. As will be explained later, a softer seal is safer than a firm, rigid seal. For instance, the rubber gasket on a flip-top bottle allows any excess $CO_2$ to escape, providing a pressure relief valve. The Brewers Association recommends that you consider using plastic screw tops instead of metal for the same reason.

If a glass bottle is being used it should be brown, not clear, to help lessen the amount of light that can potentially "skunk" or "light strike" its contents. Small neck ceramic bottles are problematic because you cannot easily see inside the bottle to check for cleanliness. Stainless steel growlers are typically large-mouth, making it easier to view the cleanliness, and light-struck beer is alleviated. There are stainless steel growlers that can be charged with $CO_2$, potentially extending the life of the product in the vessel—they are designed specifically for this purpose.

Aluminum cans (crowlers) are another option and they will maintain the carbonation level that the brewer intended. Crowlers keep light out and have some give to make up for any pressure increases. They require additional equipment to seal the lid after filling, which requires proper maintenance. Crowlers are a single-use product, recyclable, and are handy for consumers who do not want to purchase a growler. They cannot, however, be capped and reused later.

Other single-use containers are made of plastic (PET), which are typically filled using a specially designed faucet that holds the bottle in place during filling. Cardboard containers, much like a milk container with a removable cap can be tube filled. Plastic bags that have little or no oxygen and can be filled directly off the faucet are available also.

### Growler Container Cleanliness

Retailers are ultimately responsible for ensuring that any container is sanitary and "beer clean" before filling. Consumers also have a responsibility to maintain and care for growlers they own. Growler cleaning concepts mirror those outlined in the glassware cleaning section of this manual.

**Figure 6.7.** Beverage tubing (vinyl, flexible, or barrier tube) is often used to fill growlers.

- Detergents should not be fat- or oil-based.
- Proper detergent ratios should be used to ensure thorough cleaning as well as to avoid residual chemical aromas.
- A large carboy-type brush can be used to assist in cleaning; however, brushes with exposed metal at the end should not be used.
- After being thoroughly cleaned, growlers should be allowed to completely air dry and stored with the lid off.
- Cleaned growlers should be sanitized. Typical sanitizers include the trichloromelamine-, quaternary-, or iodophor-based products used for glassware.
- Pre-rinse empty growlers with cold water immediately before filling; don't fill a frozen growler.
- Establishments filling growlers should only fill containers that have been properly cleaned. In some cases, retailers require an "exchange program" where a consumer exchanges an empty, approved growler container (to be cleaned by the retailer) for a full growler.
- Local and state laws often dictate growler filling and selling practices, up to and including the requirements of pre-filled and/or pre-sealed growlers, labeling, and licensing. Retailers must familiarize themselves and comply with all local and state regulations, which can vary greatly.

### Growler Filling

Traditionally, growlers have been filled using an add-on extension tube to emulate the bottom-up filling method of a bottle filler. In most cases, these filling tubes are a specific length of flexible draught beer tubing; 3/8" ID × ½" OD vinyl tube fits the inside standard faucets. The use of a flow-control faucet to help control the flow of the beer into the growler and reduce waste is a good best practice. If a stainless steel growler fill tube is used, care must be taken to avoid damaging the inside of glass or ceramic growlers. Adding a filling tube to a standard draught system may reduce waste and filling time, but this method will increase the oxygen content of the beer, leading to rapid staling. It is possible to

**TABLE 6.1. GROWLER PRESSURE CHANGE AS FUNCTION OF TEMPERATURE**

| | Temperature | psig | barg |
|---|---|---|---|
| **Refrigerated** | 38 | 13.1 | 0.90 |
| **Cool** | 50 | 20.3 | 1.40 |
| **Room temp.** | 68 | 32.4 | 2.23 |
| **Hot day** | 100 | 57.5 | 3.96 |
| **Car interior** | 120 | 74.2 | 5.12 |

**Note:** Values assume sealed growler filled to 95% capacity with beer at 2.7 volumes $CO_2$, 5% ABV. psig, pounds per square inch, gauge; barg, bar gauge pressure

pre-purge growlers with $CO_2$, although precautions must be made for $CO_2$ exposure.

The use of a counterpressure $CO_2$ filler is another option for filling growers. Counterpressure fillers mimic the process used for commercial bottle filling. To reduce the amount of oxygen coming into contact with the beer, counterpressure systems purge most of the oxygen out of the container with $CO_2$ before filling the container with beer. It is important to make sure that the vessel being filled is rated for the pressure being used to counterpressure fill and that there is a protective shield between the operator and growler. Counterpressure systems may further reduce filling waste, but counterpressure-filled growlers will not necessarily have a longer shelf-life.

Filled growlers can shatter or explode if allowed to warm or freeze, especially if they are overfilled. The internal pressure of a filled growler warmed to room temperature (68°F) or in a hot car (90°F) may be as high as 29 psi (2 atm) or 52 psi (3.5 atm), respectively, based on a growler filled with beer at 38°F containing 2.5 volumes of $CO_2$ and sealed. Table 6.1 shows the drastic changes in pressure due to temperature change.

Growlers should be filled to the manufacturer's specified fill level. An overfilled growler can become dangerously overpressurized whereas an underfilled growler is not consumer friendly.

After filling, the growler should be rinsed off with fresh water and sealed with tape or heat shrink. A label identifying the contents of each growler (IBU, ABV, and name) should be attached. The Brewers Association has a template that can be used: https://www.brewersassociation.org/educational-publications/important-information-for-growler-tags/.

### Growler Filling Hygiene

Be prepared for the extra effort required to deliver quality beer free of off-flavors in a growler. Basic hygiene begins with draught beer lines cleaned a minimum of every two weeks as outlined by the recommendations found in this manual. Faucets and filling tubes should be rinsed, cleaned, and sanitized after each growler fill.

More complex counterpressure filling systems have a greater need for comprehensive cleaning to avoid off-flavors caused by infection. They should be cleaned at least as often as the rest of the draught system and run through a rinse cycle nightly. A well-designed and diligently executed maintenance plan will ensure hygienic, trouble-free draught system operation and fresh, flavorful beer.

**Figure 6.8.** Growler tags are available to download at https://www.BrewersAssociation.org; they include best practice tips and safety information.

## GROWLER SAFETY NOTES FOR RETAILERS AND CONSUMERS

Filled growlers can shatter or explode if allowed to warm or freeze, especially if they are overfilled. The internal pressure of a filled growler warmed to room temperature (68°F) or in a hot car (90°F) may be as high as 29 psi (2 atm) or 52 psi. (These examples assume a growler filled to 99% capacity with beer at 38°F containing 2.5 volumes $CO_2$, which is then sealed). The Brewers Association recommends:

- Only use growler containers specifically designed for packaged carbonated beer, and ask the container supplier to verify that the pressure rating is equal to or greater than the pressure from carbonation in the beer being filled. Many containers currently in use are not designed for carbonated beverages.
- If filling by counterpressure, know the pressure rating of the system used and ensure the system includes shielding between the growler being filled and people nearby in case of failure
- Do not overfill a growler. Always leave 5% head space or fill to the manufacturer's recommended fill line if one is shown.
- For growlers with threaded screw-on closures, consider using plastic rather than metal closures; plastic closures may vent more readily if overpressurization occurs; if using metal closures you may wish to discuss this issue with your supplier.
- Keep filled growlers cold and dark. Never allow a filled growler to warm or to freeze, because this can result in potentially hazardous shattering.
- Visually inspect every growler before filling. Do not fill glass or ceramic growlers with cracks or chips, those which have been engraved, or older growlers with pitted or unsmooth glass surfaces, because the pressure strength of these growlers will be significantly reduced.

### Consumer Education, Post-Filling Quality

Draught beer is a lot like bread, best when enjoyed fresh. Growlers should be consumed within 24–72 hours of filling and should be finished within hours of being opened (enjoy responsibly). In cases where growlers have been pre-filled, ensure your growler has been filled that day for optimal freshness. Brewery studies show that beer quality begins to suffer almost immediately after filling. Within 24 hours, carbonation, mouthfeel, and the hallmark flavors of the beer begin to degrade, and within 72 hours stale flavors become obvious.

Helpful hints:

- Keep filled growlers cold and dark. Remember, an increase in temperature will increase pressure and could cause a growler to burst. Light can damage beer by skunking.
- Growlers should be thoroughly cleaned, sanitized, rinsed, and allowed to air dry immediately after emptying. After cleaning, growlers should be stored with the lid off.
- Laws vary from state to state, so check before starting a program. Some states require that establishments can only fill growlers with their logo or that they have sold.
- Prerinse the growler before filling with fresh water run through a cold plate to prechill the growler prior to filling.
- Keep a container of sanitizer for the fill tubes behind the bar.
- Keep extra seals for either style cap behind the bar in case a customer brings in a different type of growler.
- Use brown bottles instead of clear glass. Brown glass will protect beer from the harmful effects of light.

For more information on growlers, search Growlers on http://www.BrewersAssociation.org. ■

7

# SYSTEM MAINTENANCE AND CLEANING

In addition to alcohol and $CO_2$, finished beer contains proteins, carbohydrates, and hundreds of other organic compounds. Yeast and bacteria routinely enter draught systems, where they feed on beer and attach to draught lines. Minerals also precipitate from beer, leaving deposits in lines and fixtures.

Within days of installing a brand new draught system, biofilm deposits begin to build up on the surfaces that come into contact with beer. Without proper cleaning, these deposits soon affect beer flavor and undermine the system's ability to dispense quality beer.

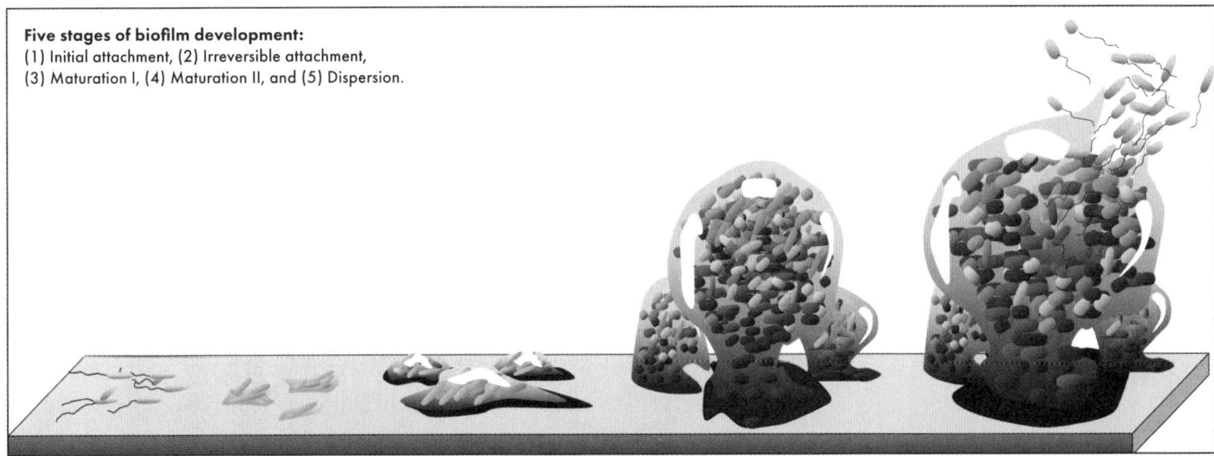


**Figure 7.1.** Biofilms can easily become established in dirty lines.
Creative Commons: D. Davis - From: D. Monroe. "Looking for Chinks in the Armor of Bacterial Biofilms". *PLoS Biology* 5 (11, e307) journals.plos.org/plosbiology/article?id=10.1371/journal.pbio.0050307.

When undertaken using proper solutions and procedures, line cleaning prevents the buildup of organic material and mineral deposits while eliminating flavor-changing microbes. Thus, a well-designed and diligently executed maintenance plan ensures trouble-free draught system operation and fresh, flavorful beer.

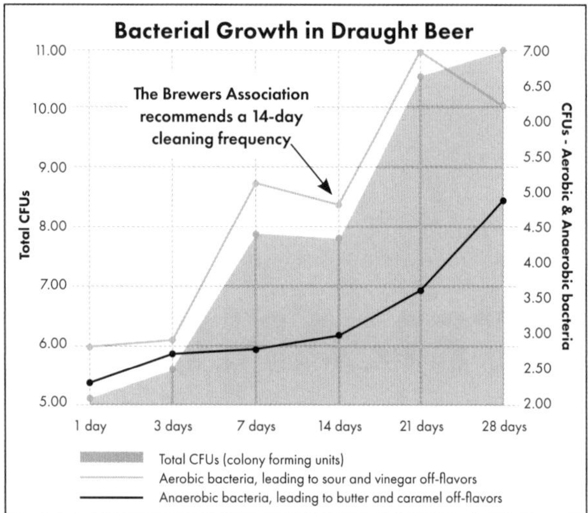


**Figure 7.2.** Bacteria can grow exponentially in uncleaned draught lines.
Graph adapted from E. Storgårds, "Microbiological Quality of Draught Beer—Is There Reason for Concern?" in Proceedings of the European Brewing Convention Symposium Draught Beer, Packaging and Dispense, Monograph XXV, Edinburgh, September 1996 (Nürnberg: Carl Getränke-Fachverlag), 92-103.

## CLEANING GUIDELINES

Many states require regular draught system line cleaning, but all too often the methods used fall short of what is needed to actually maintain beer quality. In preparing this manual, our committee polled all sectors of the beer industry and called on our own cumulative experience to determine the necessary and sufficient conditions for proper draught system maintenance. In this chapter, we recommend and detail the practices that have proven effective in sustaining the quality of beer dispensed by draught systems.

Draught line cleaning should only be performed by trained personnel.

Please note that all parts of the recommendations must be implemented. For example, the proper cleaning solution strength will not be effective if the temperature is too cold or there is insufficient contact time with the lines; the lines themselves will remain vulnerable to a rapid decline in quality if faucets and couplers are not hand-cleaned according to the recommended procedures.

As a retailer, you may or may not clean your own draught system lines, but you have a vested interest in making sure the cleaning is done properly. Clean lines make for quality draught beer that looks good, tastes great, and pours without waste.

Take the time to review the guidelines in this manual and monitor the performance of your line cleaners—no matter who they are—to ensure that your system receives the care it needs to serve you and your customers well. Simple checks, such as maintaining cleaning logs, using a straw to scrape the inside of a faucet, and checking keg couplers for visible buildup, will help to ensure your beer lines are being properly maintained and serviced.

## COMMON ISSUES

Later in this chapter, we cover the details of cleaning solutions and procedures, but first let's review some related issues. We start with an important look at safety, then briefly discuss design considerations, and wrap up with the long-term maintenance issue of line replacement.

### Cleaning Safety

Line cleaning involves working with hazardous chemicals. The following precautions should be taken:

- Cleaning personnel should be well trained in handling hazardous chemicals.
- Personal protective equipment (PPE), including rubber gloves and eye protection, should be used whenever handling line-cleaning chemicals.
- Cleaning solution suppliers are required to provide a safety data sheet (SDS) on each of their products. Cleaning personnel should have these sheets and follow their procedures while handling line-cleaning chemicals.
- When diluting chemical concentrate, always add the chemical to water and never add water to the chemical. Adding water to concentrated caustic chemical can cause a rapid increase in temperature, possible leading to violent and dangerous spattering or eruption of the chemical.

## DRAUGHT SAFETY

Personal protective equipment (PPE) should always be worn while working or handling hazardous materials.

- Proper eyewear includes splash resistant goggles, or safety glasses made from impact-resistant plastic or tempered glass with side shields or wraparound design.
- Proper hand protection includes seamless molded gloves that extend past the wrist. Choose synthetic chemical protective material (i.e., nitrile, neoprene, or butyl rubber gloves) compatible with the hazardous chemicals being used; consult safety data sheets (SDSs) and/or the glove manufacturer's compatibility charts. Do not use latex, vinyl, or partially coated fabric gloves when handling chemicals.
- Proper footwear should be waterproof/ chemical-resistant boots composed of solid rubber or rubber-impregnated fabric substrate with full enclosure of the foot. Footwear should be waterproof, slip resistant, and chemical resistant (all three properties). Leather deteriorates with corrosives and has poor waterproofing properties.

**Safe Work Practices:**

- When mixing chemical solutions, be sure to add cleaner to water, not vice versa.
- Keep the container caps on cleaners when not dispensing.
- During cleaning, set the cleaners on the floor, not on a bar top or shelf.
- Store cleaners away from consumables.
- Do not leave any cleaning job partially complete.
- Keep chemicals away from other people.
- Be aware of slip/trip hazards and notify other people in the area.

### System Design and Cleanliness

Draught system designs should always strive for the shortest possible draw length to help reduce operating challenges and line-cleaning costs. Foaming beer and other pouring problems waste beer in greater volumes as draw length increases. Line cleaning necessitates discarding beer equal to the volume of the beer lines

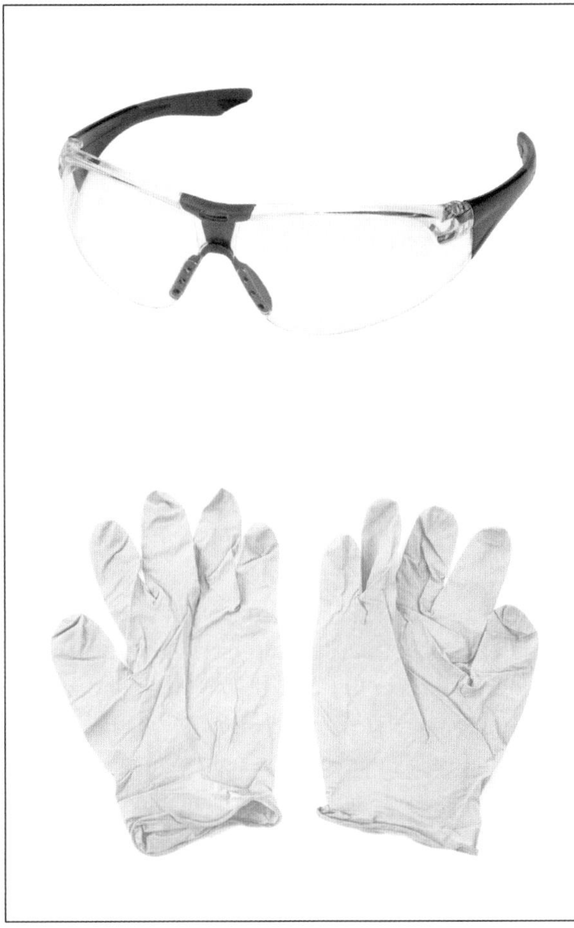

**Figure 7.3.** Personal protective equipment should include rubber gloves and eye protection. Shown here are wraparound safety glasses and nitrile gloves.

themselves. Longer runs also place a greater burden on mechanical components, increasing repair and replacement costs.

New systems should be chemically cleaned and rinsed with cold water prior to pouring beer. A system cleaning will help to eliminate potential contaminants and will remove oxygen from the lines. It is also recommended to purge all gas lines with $CO_2$ prior to tapping kegs to prevent oxygen from being pushed into fresh kegs.

One-way keg systems may require specific equipment to achieve desired cleaning methods. Split lines may also pose cleaning challenges. Be sure to check with the manufacturers of the various components in any draught beer system to ensure that all components (line materials, and all system hardware and fittings) are compatible with the cleaning methods and procedures you plan to use. The acceptable exposure limits for cleaning solution concentration, temperature, and pressure can vary by component and manufacturer.

Large venues, such as stadiums, arenas, and casinos, often combine very long draught runs with long periods of system inactivity that further complicate cleaning and maintenance. Additional maintenance costs eventually outweigh any perceived benefits of a longer system.

## OTHER LINE CLEANING METHODS

### Sponge Cleaning

Mechanical cleaning methods use sponges to physically scrub the interior of beer lines. There are advantages and disadvantages to mechanical cleaning. Potential advantages include more thorough cleaning relative to chemical cleaning alone, and time savings for draught beer cleaning service providers. Potential disadvantages include possible abrasion of the smooth beer line interior over time due to scrubbing by the sponge, and fittings or beer line that are too small in diameter, resulting in possible stuck sponges. Mechanical cleaning should only be used in draught systems that have been specifically designed to be cleaned in this way.

### Sonic Cleaning

Devices that purport to electrically or sonically clean draught lines are not a suitable substitute for chemical line cleaning. Although some sonic cleaners may inhibit bacteria and yeast growth, they have little or no cleaning effect on draught system hardware and fittings. The efficacy of sonic cleaners can be affected by the beer style and length of system, and can be interrupted by metal components in the system, such as faucets and couplers. Sonic cleaners may add some benefit to deter certain types of bacteria while having little to no effect on others. A maximum two-week chemical line cleaning cycle is recommended on all draught systems regardless of the use of a sonic cleaner.

### Automatic Cleaning Systems

All "automatic" cleaning systems or clean-in-place (CIP) systems should be able to achieve all recommendations included in this chapter, including a maximum two-week cleaning cycle, 15 minutes of recirculation, and disassembly and detailing of all hardware.

### Line Replacement and Materials

Replacing lines in your draught system at recommended intervals is an important part of draught system maintenance. Here are some general guidelines concerning line replacement and materials:

- All vinyl jumpers and vinyl direct-draw lines should be replaced every one to two years or anytime there is a bacterial or flavor contamination.
- Some suppliers have developed improved alternatives to flexible tubing that could allow for less frequent change-outs. At the time of writing, it is too early to set specific parameters and it is recommended to consult the manufacturer's recommendations.
- All long-draw trunk line should be replaced in the following instances:
  - when the system is 10 or more years old;
  - when flavor changes are imparted in a beer's draught line from an adjacent draught line;
  - when any line chronically induces flavor changes in beer.
- Beer lines may need to be replaced after pouring root beer, flavored beers, margaritas, wines, or ciders. Such beverages may permanently contaminate a draught line and possibly adjacent draught lines in the same bundle. Such contamination precludes future use of that draught line for beer.
- In the case where a coupler's gas backflow valve (check valve) is or ever has been missing, the gas line may have been compromised and should be replaced.
- Ensure the material used in the manufacture of the beer lines is compatible with the chemicals, dilution rates, and temperatures outlined in this chapter (also see "Beer Line" in chapter 1).

## DETAILED RECOMMENDATIONS

Time, temperature, mechanical action, and chemicals (including chemical concentration) are the four interdependent factors that determine draught system cleaning effectiveness. These four factors are known as the "Sinner's Circle," represented in figure 7.5. If one factor is reduced, the loss must be compensated for by increasing one or more other factors. For example, if mechanical action is lost because a recirculation pump is not used, the chemical concentration and contact time may need to be increased to account for the loss. Throughout this chapter, these four interdependent factors will be referenced.

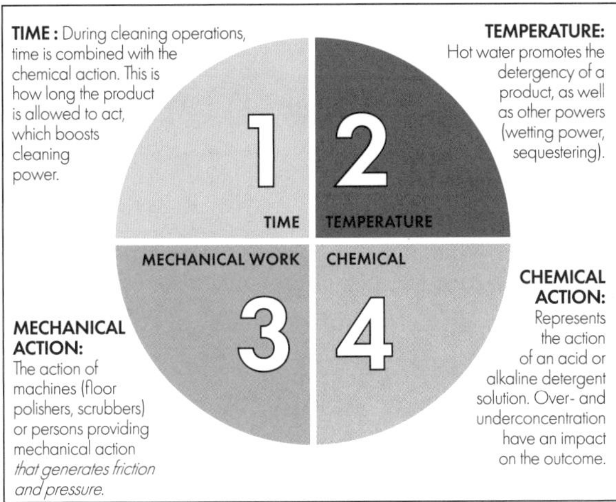


**Figure 7.5.** Effective draught system cleaning depends on four interdependent factors, arranged here as the "Sinner's Circle."

The following sections detail more specific recommendations on draught line cleaning. We begin with the basic issue of tasks and their frequency, then move into the more involved questions of cleaning solutions and procedures. The final pages of this chapter detail the procedures for cleaning with an electric recirculation pump and pressurized cleaning canister.

### Cleaning Frequency and Tasks

These are standard recommendations no matter how much or how little beer is dispensed through the system. Bacteria is constantly growing, and stronger biofilms will take hold when less frequent cleanings are practiced. More aggressive cleaning schedules and practices may be needed for older systems, problematic systems, or when proper line cleaning practices have historically not been in place.

Every two weeks (14 days):

- Draught lines should be cleaned with a caustic line-cleaning chemical following the procedures outlined in this chapter.
- All faucets should be completely disassembled and cleaned.
- All keg couplers should be scrubbed clean.
- All FOB devices (a.k.a. beer savers, foam detectors) should be cleaned in-line. Chemicals should be purged through the FOB and vented out of the FOB drain hose.

Quarterly (every three months):

- Draught beer lines should be de-stoned with an acid line-cleaning chemical or a strong chelator that is added to or as part of the alkaline chemical formulation. (The Draught Beer Quality Subcommittee is working with brewing industry researchers to complete further studies on line-cleaning chemistry, including additives such as ethylenediaminetetraacetic acid, or **EDTA**.)

Semi-annually (every six months):

- All FOB devices should be completely disassembled and hand-detailed (cleaned).
- All couplers should be completely disassembled and hand-detailed.

**Figure 7.6.** Proper PPE is necessary to prevent injury while cleaning lines.

Photo © Aaron Colussi

## CLEANING SOLUTIONS AND THEIR USAGE

### Caustic-Based Cleaners

Caustic chemicals remove organic material from the interior of draught lines, hardware, and fittings. The removal of organic material buildup prevents the growth of beer-spoiling bacteria such as *Lactobacillus*, *Pediococcus*, *Pectinatus*, and *Acetobacter*. The following are guidelines on the use of caustic chemicals.

- Use a caustic cleaner specifically designed for draught line cleaning that uses either **sodium hydroxide**, **potassium hydroxide**, or a combination of both.
- Routine use of caustic line-cleaning chemical products that are "built" with EDTA or other chelating agents may help remove calcium oxalate (beer stone) from draught lines. Brewery testing has indicated that these additives can provide significant cleaning benefits.
- Never use solutions that contain any amount of chlorine for regular system maintenance. Testing indicates that properly formulated caustic-based cleaners without chlorine can be just as effective at cleaning draught beer lines. Chlorine is not compatible with some beer line materials, and residual chlorine can cause flavor changes in draught beer.
- Based on brewery and independent lab testing, we recommend mixing caustic-based line cleaning solutions to a working strength of at least 2% **caustic** (as sodium hydroxide). A 3% caustic solution is more appropriate for problem systems, heavily soiled systems, systems with older lines, or for any line that imparts a flavor change to the beer served from it. Chemical manufacturers should provide detailed mixing instructions on the bottle for 2% and 3% caustic solutions. If this information is not available, contact your chemical manufacturer to determine how much chemical is needed to achieve these recommended concentrations.
- We recommend the use of portable titration kits to confirm the working caustic strength of beer line-cleaning solutions (fig. 7.7).
- Mix caustic solution with water warmed to a temperature between 80°F and 110°F.
- Caustic cleaner must remain in contact with the draught line for at least:
  - 15 minutes when solution is being recirculated, or
  - 20 minutes for static or pressure canister cleaning.
- Caustic and acid should always be separate and never come into contact with each other.

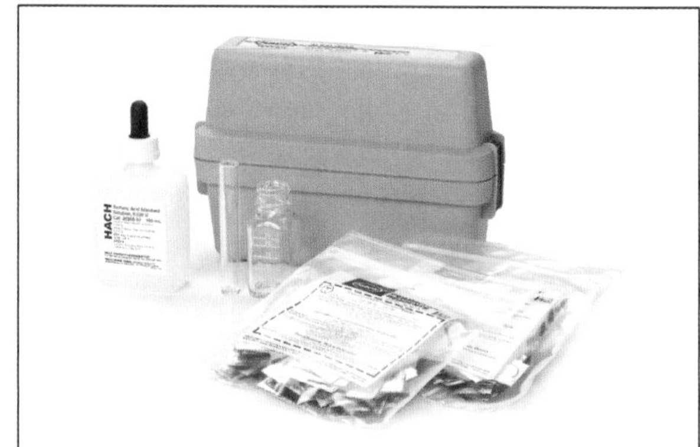

**Figure 7.7.** Portable titration kit.

Photo courtesy of Hach Company

### Acid-Based Cleaners

Acid-based line-cleaner chemicals remove inorganic materials, such as calcium oxalate (beer stone) and calcium carbonate (**water stone**), from the interior of draught lines, hardware, and fittings. The following are guidelines on the use of **acid cleaners**.

- Routine use of caustic cleaning solutions with EDTA or other chelating agent additives can help reduce calcium oxalate buildup in draught lines, which may decrease the need to clean regularly with an acid-based cleaner.
- Acid-based line cleaners suitable for draught line cleaning contain solutions of phosphoric acid.
- Some acid-based cleaners use acids that can harm your draught equipment:
  - Hydrochloric acid corrodes stainless steel and should not be used for cleaning draught lines.
  - Nitric acid is not compatible with nylon products, including some commonly used draught line tubing, and should not be used for cleaning draught lines.
- Mix acid-based line cleaner to the solution strength recommended by the manufacturer.
- Mix acid-based line cleaner with water warmed to a temperature between 80°F and 110°F.
- Acid solution must remain in contact with the draught line for at least:
  - 15 minutes when solution is being recirculated, or
  - 20 minutes for static or pressure canister cleaning.

- Acid cleanings should be in addition to, not in place of, caustic cleanings.
- Caustic and acid should always be separate and never come into contact with each other.

### Water Rinsing

Rinsing with fresh water is an important part of chemical line cleaning. The following are guidelines on rinsing draught systems correctly to ensure proper cleaning and safety.

- Always flush draught lines with fresh water *before* pumping chemical into the line.
- Always flush draught lines with water *after* using any chemical solution (caustic and acid).
- Acid and caustic should NEVER be mixed in line or in a common bucket. Between chemical cleanings a draught system should be flushed with water until pH neutral.
- Continue water flushing until:
  - no solid matter appears in the rinse water;
  - no cleaning chemical residue remains in the draught line.
- Confirm the removal of cleaning chemicals by testing the solution with pH strips or a pH meter.
  - Before beginning the rinse, draw a reference sample of tap water and test its pH.
  - During rinsing, periodically test the rinse water exiting the draught system.
  - When the pH of the rinse water matches that of the tap water, the chemical is fully flushed out.
- *Chemical cleaning solutions must never be flushed from draught lines with beer.*

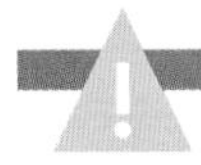

## DRAUGHT SAFETY

Used cleaner solutions can be either highly alkaline or highly acidic, and likely contain high concentrations of organic material. Thus, used cleaner solutions can be hazardous to put down the drain. The technician should become familiar with local laws and sewer capabilities before disposing of the waste water.

## CLEANING METHODS AND PROCEDURES

Because every draught beer system is different, there is no definitive procedure for cleaning them. There are, however, certain principles that apply to cleaning every system. To be effective, cleaning solutions need to reach every inch of beer line and every nook and cranny of the connectors and hardware. You can hand-clean some items, like couplers and faucets, but most of the system must be reached by fluid flowing through the beer lines. The industry currently uses two cleaning procedures for beer lines: recirculation by electric pump, and static or pressurized canister cleaning.

Electric recirculating pump cleaning is recommended as the preferred method for nearly all systems. Recirculation pump cleaning uses a combination of chemical cleaning and mechanical action to effectively clean a draught system by increasing the normal flow rate through the beer lines during the cleaning process.

While cleaning with a pressurized canister is an alternative, it is significantly less efficient and effective and is only recommended when recirculation cleaning is not possible. Pressure pot cleaning requires additional time (usually a minimum of 20 minutes) and steps to ensure that the cleaning solutions have the right contact time in the line, which makes up for the lack of mechanical force. Pressurized cleaning canisters may also require a higher concentration of cleaner, because the $CO_2$ pressurizing the canister can neutralize or reduce the effectiveness of the caustic chemical.

When using a cleaning canister, ensure all recommendations outlined in the "Pressurized Cleaning Canister Step-By-Step Procedure" section are followed. Cleaning canisters often require multiple trips to and from the cooler and the need to continually refill the canister to completely fill all draught lines throughout the system. Cleaning canisters also need to be filled and additional trips to a cooler need to be made for both the water prerinse and post-rinse. On average, when cleaning with a recirculation pump a technician will need to make 2–3 round trips between the cooler and the bar. When properly cleaning with a pressurized cleaning canister, 5–6 round trips need to be made between the cooler and the bar.

The following sections cover these two cleaning methods, starting with setup and proceeding to the detailed steps for each procedure.

### Before You Start

Regardless of your cleaning method, some system designs require specific attention before you begin cleaning. Here's a list of items to check and consider. If using an electric recirculation pump, you should also refer to the "Unusual Situations When Cleaning with a Recirculation Pump" section on page 74 for more details.

- In pneumatic beer pump systems:
  - turn off the gas supply to the pumps;
  - on the line(s) to be back-flushed, set the pump valve or flow diverter orientation to "backflush" so that cleaning solution may flow through the pump body in the appropriate direction as needed.
- All legs in split lines (lines that are "Y'd" in the cooler or under the bar to feed more than one faucet from a single keg) must be cleaned as completely separate draught lines.

## ELECTRIC RECIRCULATING PUMP CLEANING

### Key Considerations When Setting Up

- The chemical flow should be the reverse of the beer flow wherever possible. Ideally, the flow direction should be alternated between cleanings.
- Ideal chemical flow rate achieves twice the flow rate of the beer. In standard systems, beer flows at 1 gal./min., so ideal chemical flow rate is 2 gal./min. A 2 gal./min. flow rate may not be attainable for all systems. In these cases, a minimum of 1 gal./min. should be achieved.

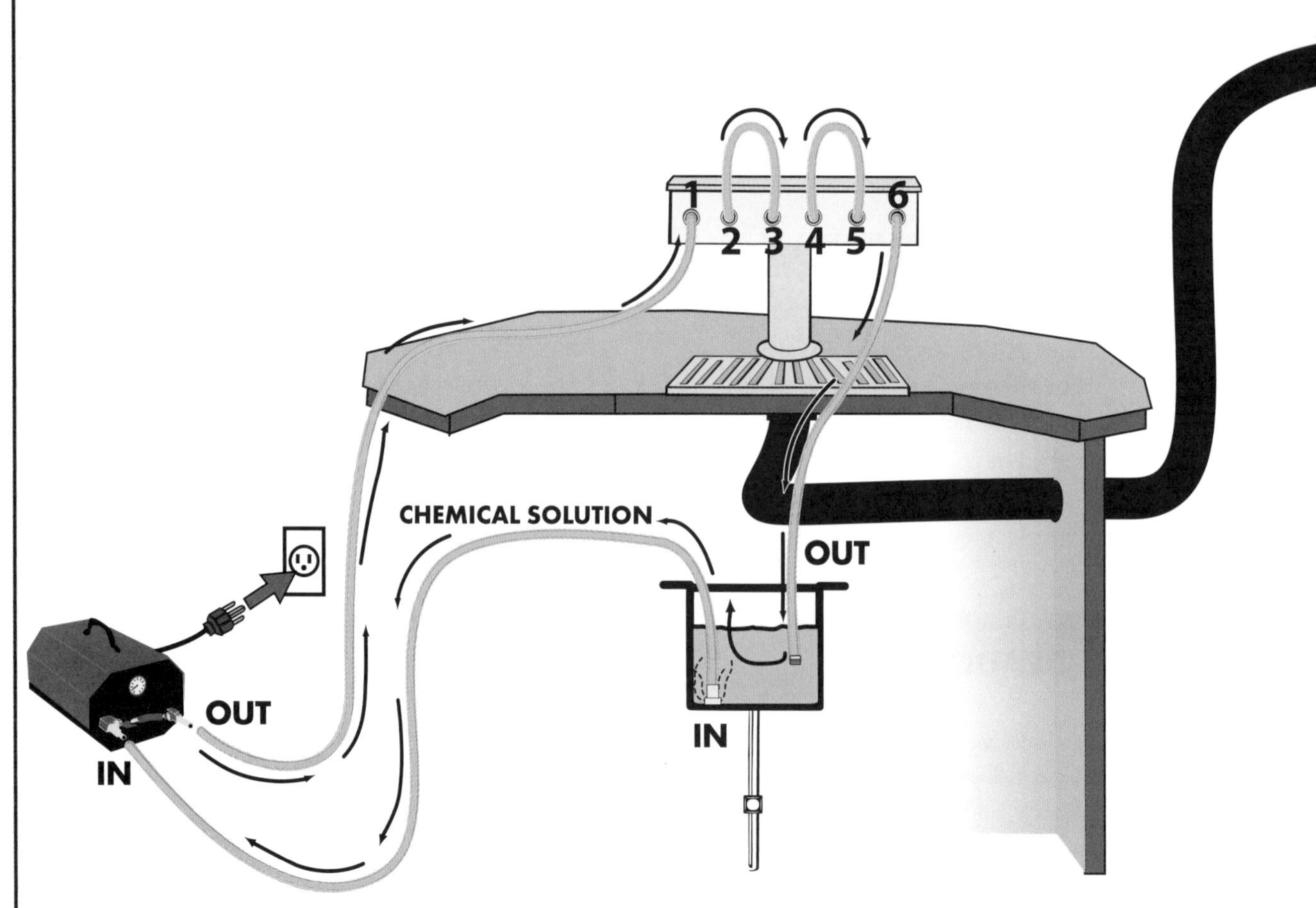


**Figure 7.8.** Typical line cleaning setup with electric pump recirculation.

- The flow rate can be controlled by:
  - minimizing the number of draught lines cleaned at one time, or
  - increasing the size of the pump used without exceeding the working pressure of the draught system.
- The flow rate can be tested by measuring the volume dispensed in 15 seconds. Multiply this volume by 4 to determine the flow rate in ounces or gallons per minute (1 gal. = 128 fl. oz.).
- The back-pressure on the draught system during recirculation should never exceed 50 psi.
- Under these conditions, the chemical solution should recirculate for a minimum of 15 minutes.
- The recirculation pump should be primed prior to connecting the pump to the draught system by running water through the pump, the inlet hose, and the outlet hose. Priming the pump will reduce the resistance caused by pushing air through the system.

### Electric Recirculation Pump Cleaning Step-By-Step Procedure

1. Begin by connecting two keg couplers with a cleaning adapter or cleaning cup. Cleaning adapters are available to accommodate many different combinations of coupler types, with the most common being "D" type to "D" type, as shown in figure 7.11 and 7.12. Do not engage the couplers or else cleaning solution may travel up the gas line. The shaft on each side of the adapter raises the check ball within the coupler (see fig. 1.9 on page 9) to allow cleaning solution to flow in either direction.

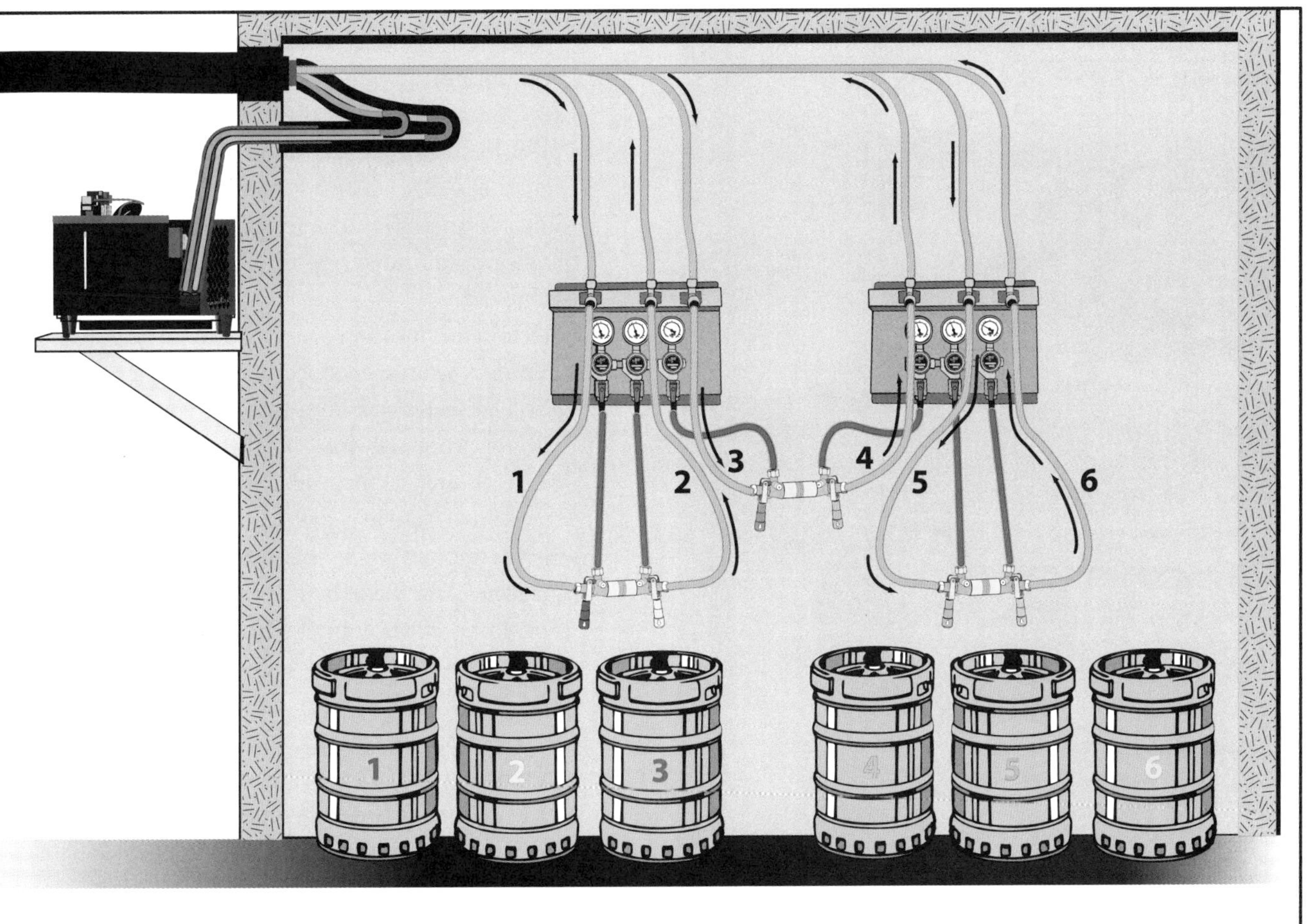

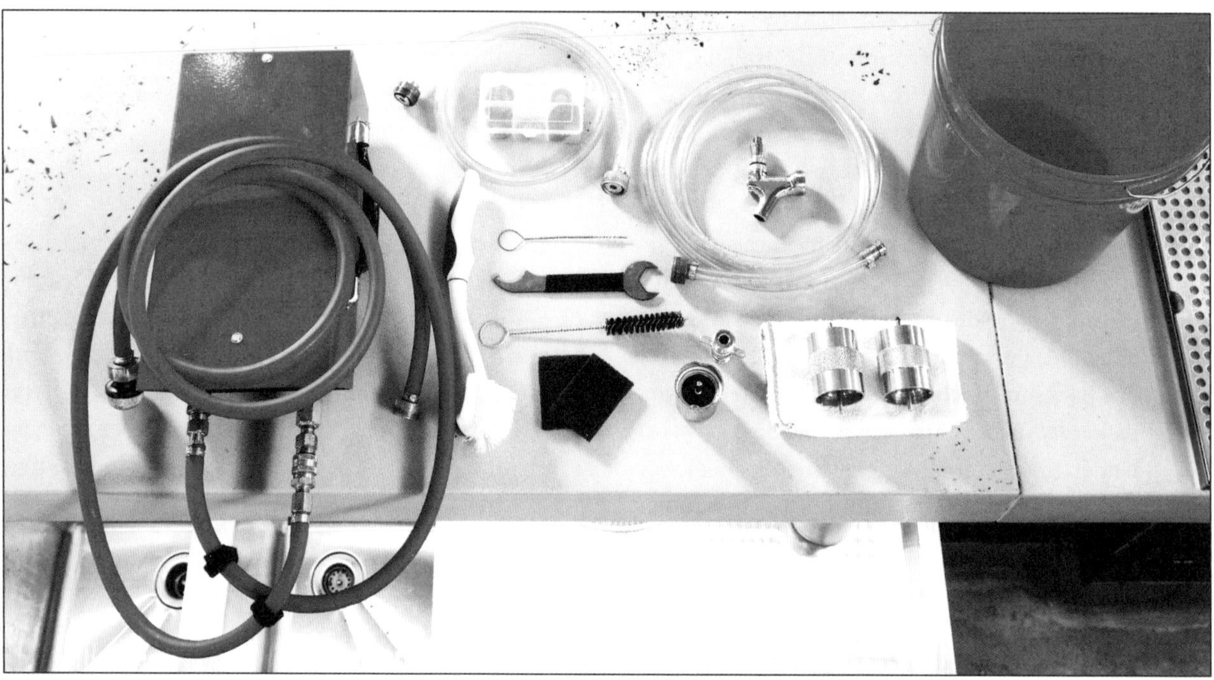

**Figure 7.9.** Recirculation pump equipment.

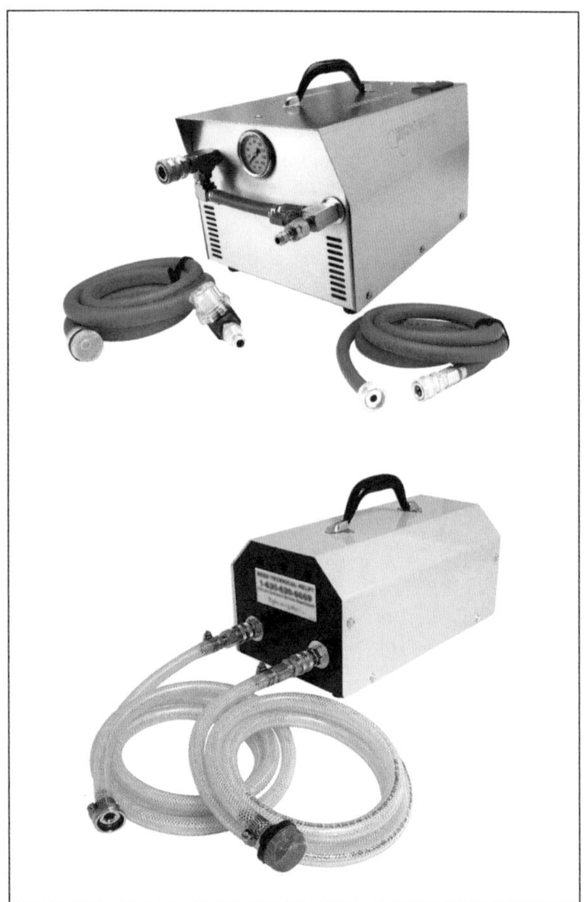

**Figure 7.10.** Examples of electric recirculation pumps.

Photos © Aaron Colussi

   a. If cleaning four lines, connect a second set of lines with another cleaning coupler, creating a second "loop" (*see* fig. 7.8 on p. 68–69). Cleaning more than four lines at once should only be done when a minimum flow rate of 1 gal./min. is achieved.
   b. To clean the lines and couplers used for kegs in series, begin by connecting the couplers attached to the gas lines (i.e., the couplers farthest from the faucet). Then, attach a cap with a check-ball lifter to each of the couplers that are in series.
2. On the corresponding lines at the bar, remove both faucets from their shanks (fig. 7.13).
   a. For loops with long and/or numerous lines, prime the pump by filling the pump and pump jumper lines completely with water before attaching the outlet hose to the shank (fig. 7.14).
   b. When cleaning two lines, attach the outlet hose from the pump to one shank and a drain hose or spare faucet to the other shank.
   c. When cleaning four lines, attach the outlet hose from the pump to one shank,

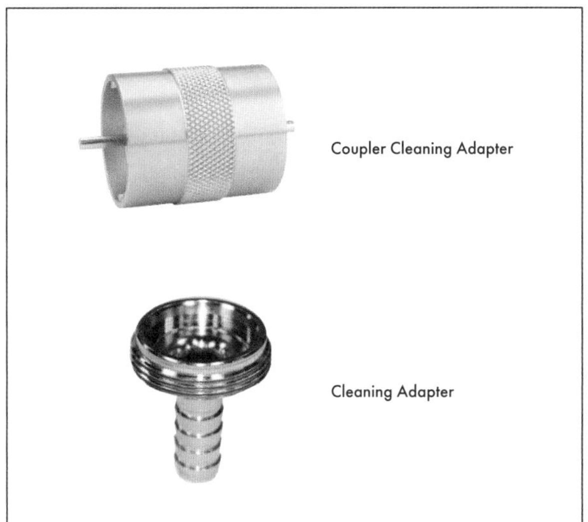


**Figure 7.11.** Typical line cleaning adapters.

**Figure 7.13.** Faucets should be removed and cleaned separately.

**Figure 7.12.** Couplers can be linked to aid in recirculation cleaning.

**Figure 7.14.** Ensure that all hoses are connected securely before cleaning.

connect the other shank in the loop to a shank in the second loop using a jumper hose fitted with a cleaning adapter on each end, and attach a drain hose or spare faucet to the remaining shank in the second loop. When cleaning four lines, ensure that the drain hose and outlet hose from the pump are not on the same coupler loop.

3. Fill a bucket (the "water bucket") with warm water and place the inlet hose into the water. Turn the pump on and flush beer into a second bucket (the "chemical bucket") until the line runs clear with water. Shut the pump off and discard the flushed beer.
4. Turn the pump back on, allowing warm water to run into the clean chemical bucket. Measure the flow rate of the liquid by filling a beer pitcher or some container with a known volume. A steady flow rate that ideally exceeds the flow rate of the beer is recommended. If cleaning is configured for four lines and flow rate is too slow, remove the jumpers and clean each pair of lines separately.

- Allow the chemical bucket to fill with just enough water to cover the inlet hose of the pump.
- Add the appropriate amount of line cleaning

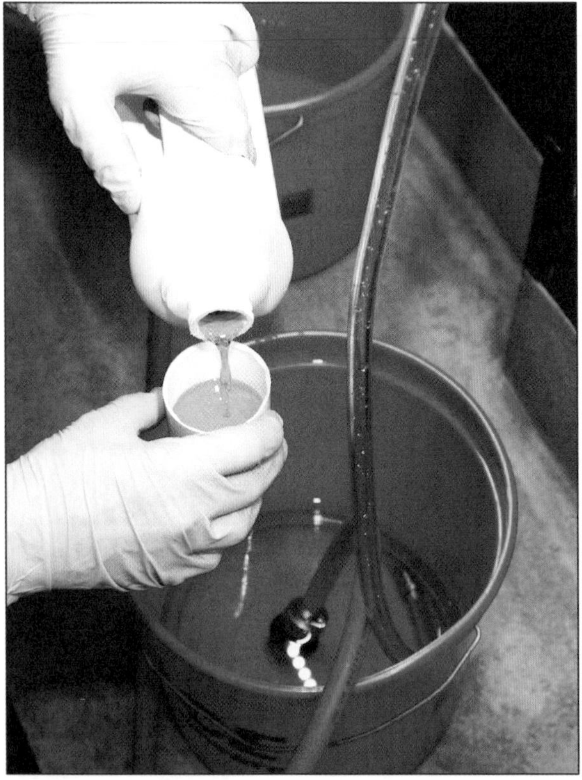

Figure 7.15. Ensure that cleaning solution is added so as to achieve the correct strength.

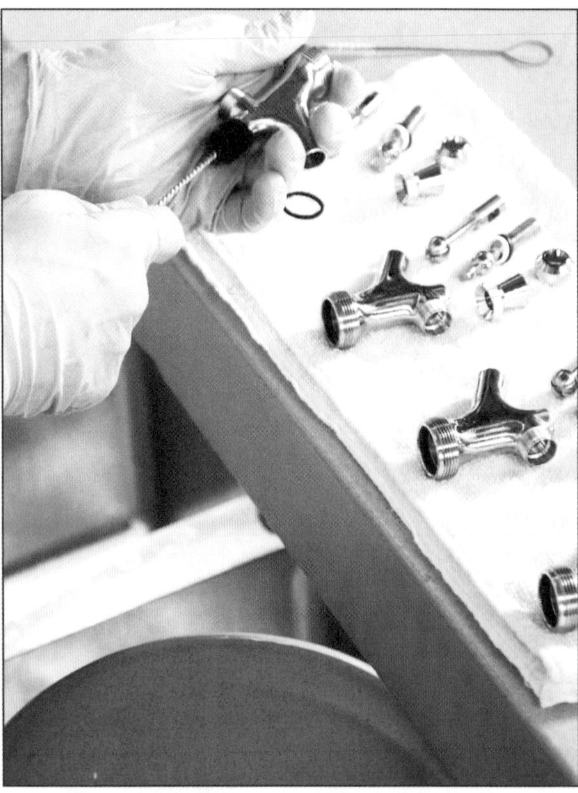

Figure 7.16. Faucets should be cleaned every time lines are cleaned.

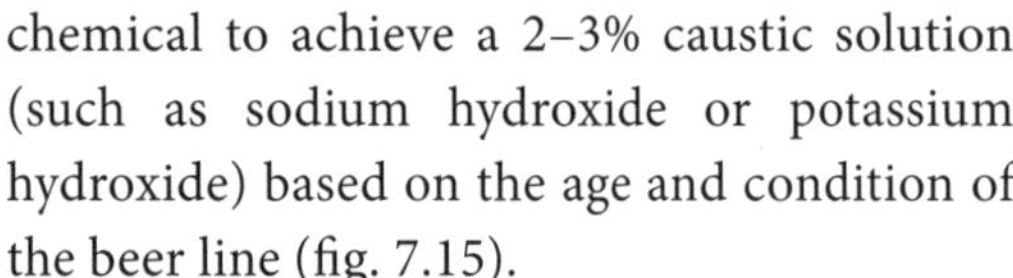

chemical to achieve a 2–3% caustic solution (such as sodium hydroxide or potassium hydroxide) based on the age and condition of the beer line (fig. 7.15).

- Enough line cleaning chemical should be added to distribute throughout the water in the entire draught system, including the water in the chemical bucket.
- The total amount of water in the system can be estimated by the amount of water needed to clear the beer out of the system.

5. Remove the inlet hose from the water bucket and place it into the chemical bucket. There should now be a closed loop. The cleaning solution should be draining into the same bucket that the pump is pulling from (fig. 7.8).
6. Allow the cleaning solution to recirculate for a minimum of 15 minutes. While waiting:

- Purge the circulating cleaning solution through FOB devices and ensure FOBs are filled with cleaning solution and vented out of the FOB drain hose.
- Clean your faucets (fig. 7.16).
- Fill the water bucket with cold water.

7. Begin your rinse by removing the inlet hose from the chemical bucket and placing it into the water bucket (now filled with cold water).
8. Continue pumping cold water from the water bucket into the chemical bucket (shutting off the pump and dumping the chemical bucket as needed) until all the cleaning solution has been pushed out of the draught lines and there is no solid matter in the rinse water. Use pH paper to verify all cleaning chemicals have been rinsed away.
9. Finish up by shutting off the pump, detaching the cleaning coupler, and replacing the faucets.

When finished:

10. Be sure to return all system components to their original functional settings; for example, turn on gas supply to pneumatic beer pumps, and reset FOBs and pneumatic pump flow diverters.

## PRESSURIZED CLEANING CANISTER

### Key Considerations

While cleaning with a pressurized canister is an alternative to cleaning with a recirculation pump, it is significantly less efficient and effective and is only recommended when recirculation cleaning is not possible. This procedure requires additional time and steps to ensure that the cleaning solutions have the right contact time in the beer line to make up for the lack of mechanical force.

### Pressurized Cleaning Canister Step-By-Step Procedure

1. Fill the cleaning canister with clean water.
2. Untap the keg and tap the cleaning canister. Engage the coupler.
   a. To clean the lines and couplers used for kegs in series, begin by connecting the couplers attached to the gas lines (i.e., the couplers farthest from the faucet). Then, attach a cap with a check-ball lifter to each of the couplers that are in series. Open faucet until the beer is flushed out and clear water is pouring.
3. Untap the canister and fill the canister with the cleaning chemical mixed to yield a 2–3% caustic solution (for example, sodium hydroxide or potassium hydroxide), depending on the age and condition of your beer line.
4. Tap the canister again. *Please note:* When applying $CO_2$ to a pressurized cleaning canister containing a caustic cleaning solution, the $CO_2$ will weaken or neutralize the caustic solution. It is best not to agitate or let the caustic solution stand in the same container for an extended period. For the same reason, the use of cleaning canisters that feature a "spitting" action, whereby $CO_2$ is injected directly into the outflow of solution, is not recommended.
5. Open the faucet until the water is flushed out and cleaning solution is pouring from the faucet.
6. Shut off the faucet. At this point, it has been common practice that the canister is untapped and faucets are removed and cleaned. This practice is NOT recommended. By releasing the pressure from the system, some of the cleaning solution will leak from the system, preventing the cleaning solution from contacting the high points of the system.
7. Return to the cooler and purge cleaning solution through FOB devices and ensure FOBs are filled with cleaning solution and vented out of the FOB drain hose.
8. Allow cleaning solution and beer line to be in contact for no less than 20 minutes.
9. Untap the canister.
   a. If the system is driven with pneumatic beer pumps, shut off the gas supply to the pumps to turn them off.
10. Remove the faucet and clean.
11. Replace faucet.
12. Empty, rinse, and fill the canister with clean, cold water and retap.
13. Open the faucet and rinse until all cleaning solution has been flushed out and there is no solid matter in the rinse water. Use pH paper to verify all cleaning chemicals have been rinsed away.

**DRAUGHT SAFETY**

The best way to ensure complete rinsing of all chemical residue is by checking the pH, which can be done very affordably with test strips. Your line cleaner supplier should be able to provide pH test strips. The pH of caustic cleaner should be 10–13.5; the pH of acid cleaner should be 2–4. When a system is completely rinsed, the pH of the rinse water should be equal to that of the local tap water.

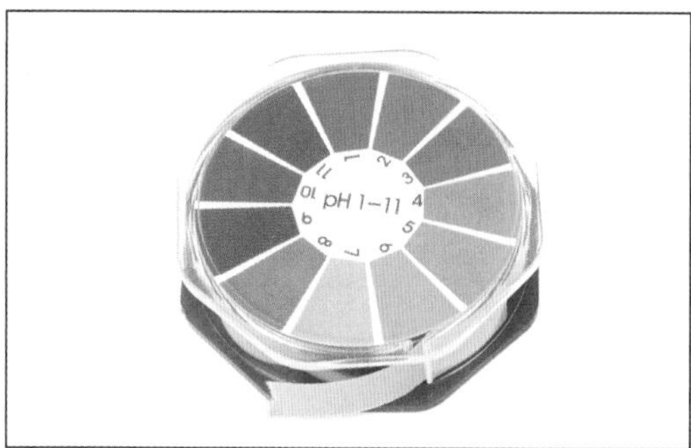


**Figure 7.18.** pH test strips, or pH paper, can be used to test that all cleaning chemicals have been rinsed from your draught system.

Photos © Getty/theJIPEN (pH test strip); Aaron Colussi (cleaning)

14. Finish by untapping the canister, retapping the keg, and pouring beer until it dispenses clear.

When finished:

15. Be sure to return all system components to their original functional settings; for example, turn on gas supply to pneumatic beer pumps, and reset FOBs and pneumatic pump flow diverters.

## UNUSUAL SITUATIONS WHEN CLEANING WITH A RECIRCULATION PUMP

Cleaning with an electric recirculation pump is recommended as the preferred method for nearly all systems. However, at times the system design can inhibit the ability to effectively clean with a recirculation pump. The following is a guide for cleaning more complex systems when using a recirculation pump.

### Pneumatic Beer Pumps

Pneumatic beer pumps are not multi-directional, so pushing cleaning solution through a pump in the reverse direction is not possible without appropriate modifications. Beer pumps should be installed with flow-reversal valves that allow for recirculation cleaning. Some beer pumps without existing flow-reversal valves allow the valve to be added onto the existing pump. Other beer pumps may require inline quick-disconnect fittings (fig. 7.20) to be installed to reverse the liquid flow. In no cases should the cleaning solution bypass the beer pump.

**Figure 7.19.** Beer pump flow-reversal valve.

### Split or Y'd Lines

The preferred method to clean split lines (or Y'd lines) is to clean each tower as its own separate system. This allows each system to get a complete recirculation clean. When using this method, it is important that the entire system is rinsed at the same time to ensure no residual chemical is caught in a split line.

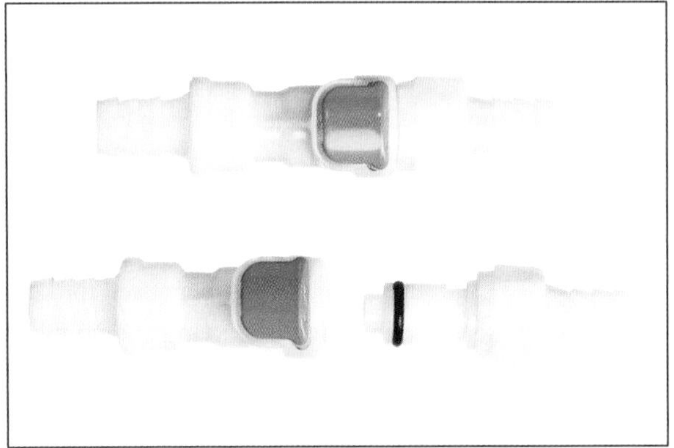

**Figure 7.20.** In-line quick-disconnect fittings.

An alternative, but less effective, way of cleaning split lines is to set up recirculation cleaning on one tower and draw liquid through the remaining split towers. When using this method, a traditional recirculation cleaning is setup on one tower using a larger 3–5 gal. "chemical bucket." The chemical bucket should be nearly filled with 2–3% caustic cleaning solution. Using an empty bucket of the same size, cleaning solution will be drawn through the split lines into the empty bucket while simultaneously depleting the chemical bucket. Be sure to leave enough caustic cleaning solution in your primary chemical bucket to maintain recirculation. This step is repeated for each step of the cleaning process, including water prerinse, cleaning solution, and water post-rinse. Because the split lines are receiving less mechanical action than the recirculation lines, additional time or a 3% caustic cleaning solution may be needed to make up for the loss of mechanical action (*see* fig. 7.5 on p.65).

### Challenging Cooler Connections

Equipment manufacturers make a variety of cleaning flushers that allow for connecting couplers of two different system types (fig. 7.22). Custom cleaning flushers can also be built using various components (fig. 7.23).

Photos © Aaron Colussi (quick-disconnect and three-way fittings)

Building custom couplers allows for connections between couplers of different system types without having to rely on ready-built flushers. In addition, custom lengths of vinyl tubing can be added between components to assist in making connections across large coolers.

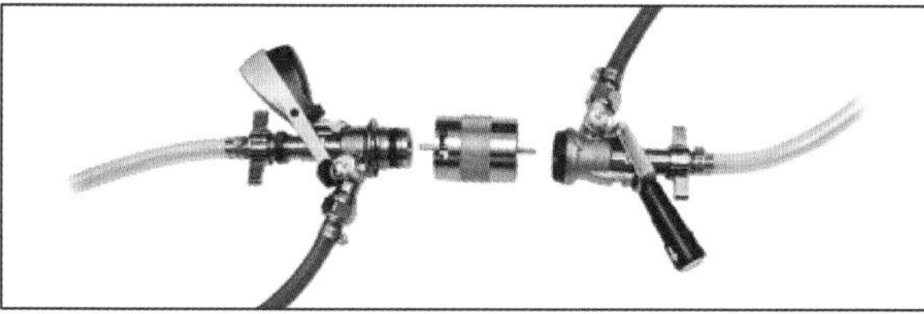

**Figure 7.22.** Cleaning flusher coupler connectors allow two different coupler systems to be connected. Shown here is a flusher that allows a "D" or "S" system to connect to a "U" system coupler.

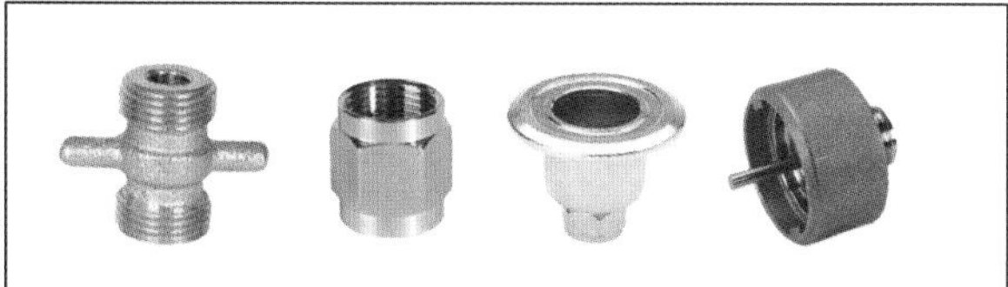

**Figure 7.23.** Example fittings for constructing custom cleaning adapters. The components pictured would connect a "D" or "S" system to an "A" system coupler.

Similar components can also be used to design three-way coupler cleaning adapters (fig. 7.24). Traditional recirculation pump cleaning systems use an even number of lines to create the recirculation loop. A three-way coupler allows for an odd number of lines to be connected by utilizing two drain lines.

A single-line direct draw can also be cleaned by setting up a loop within the one line.

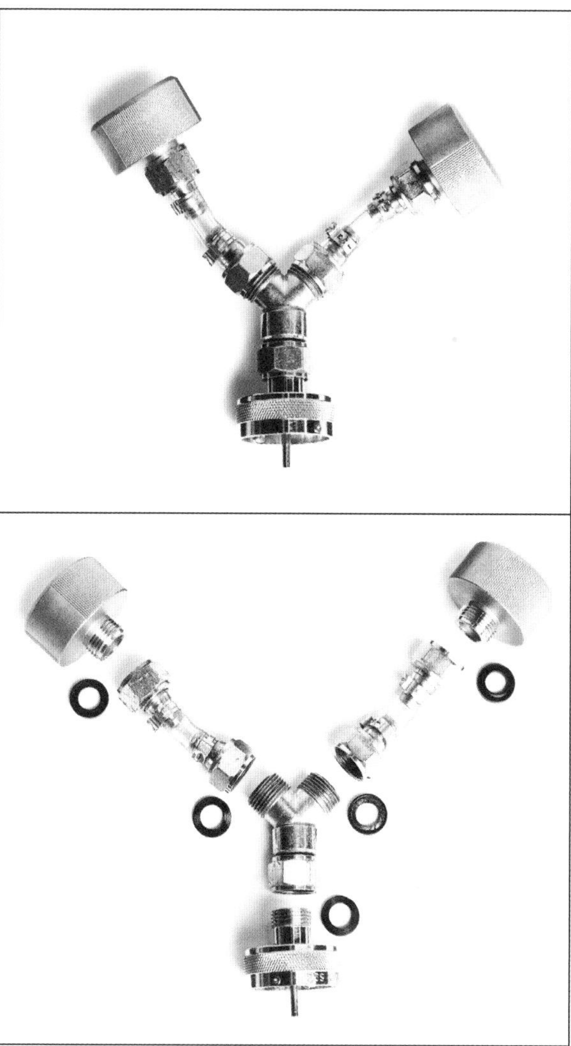

**Figure 7.24.** Example fittings for constructing a three-way cleaning adapter.

## TESTING FOR CLEANLINESS

The following are a few of the most common ways to test for draught system cleanliness.

### Sensory Evaluation

A thorough sensory evaluation by a trained taster can reveal signs of bacterial infection in a draught system. (Refer to chapter 8 for a list of off-flavors and their corresponding bacteria.) However, bacterial contamination begins long before it can be detected by human senses. Draught system maintenance is inherently preventive, designed to prevent bacterial contamination from taking hold. If only sensory evaluations are used for testing, it may be too late by the time bacteria reveal themselves through detectable tastes and aromas.

**Figure 7.25.** Sensory evaluation is a useful tool to ensure proper cleanliness in a draught system.

### ATP Testing

ATP testing can be a convenient and portable way to test for cleanliness in the field. The ATP test is a process of rapidly measuring for the presence of actively growing microorganisms through the detection of adenosine triphosphate (ATP) using a luminometer (fig. 7.26). While ATP testing can be an indicator of cleanliness, it is unable to differentiate between beer-spoiling organisms and other naturally occurring, less worrisome organic material such as yeast.

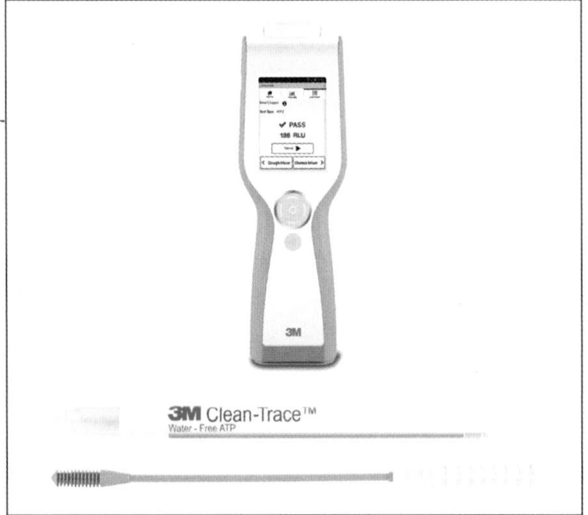


**Figure 7.26.** ATP testing equipment can be used to verify line-cleaning effectiveness by sampling rinse water.

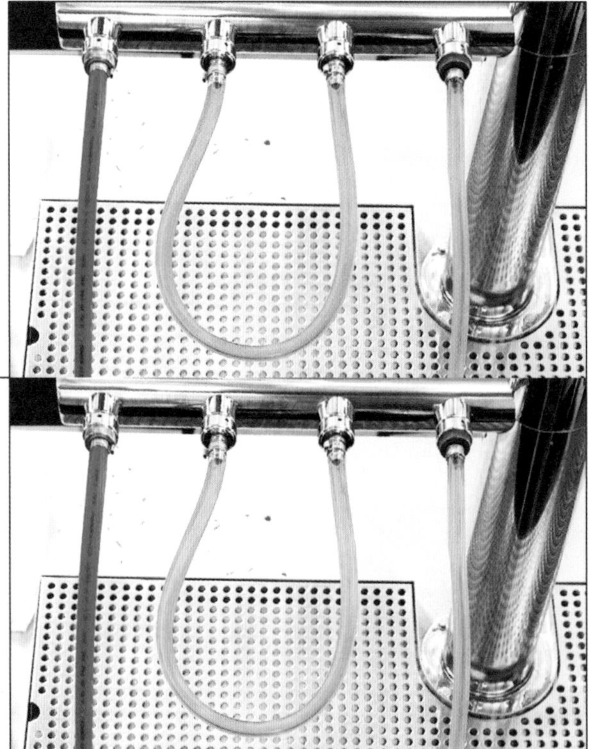

**Figure 7.27.** Color indicators can be used to test draught system cleanliness. Thonhauser's DESANA™ MAX system changes color, from green to purple, to indicate cleanliness.

### Color Indicators

Some chemical manufacturers have color-changing chemicals that can provide indicators of a draught system's cleanliness (fig. 7.27). Similar to ATP testing, these methods are only an indicator of cleanliness and are unable to differentiate between beer-spoiling organisms and other naturally occurring, less worrisome organic material.

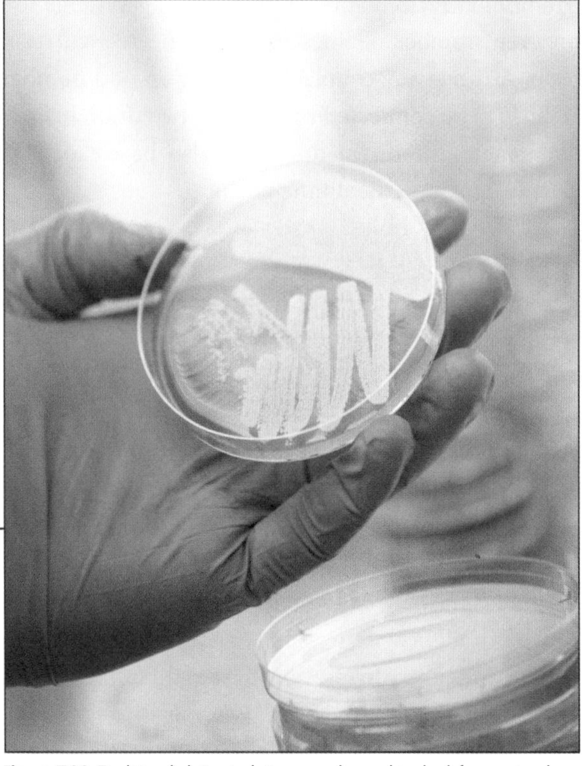

**Figure 7.28.** Traditional plating techniques can be used to check for yeast and bacteria contamination in draught lines.

### Plating

Taking samples, plating on media, and growing microbial colonies is the only way to truly identify specific microorganisms that are growing in a draught system (fig 7.28). Plating and interpreting samples can identify each type of microbial species and how prevalent it is. Unfortunately, this process is cumbersome in the field, time-consuming, and costly.

Photos Reproduced with permission © 3M 2019. All rights reserved; © Aaron Colussi (color change, inspecting) © www.johnjohnstoncreative.com (plating)

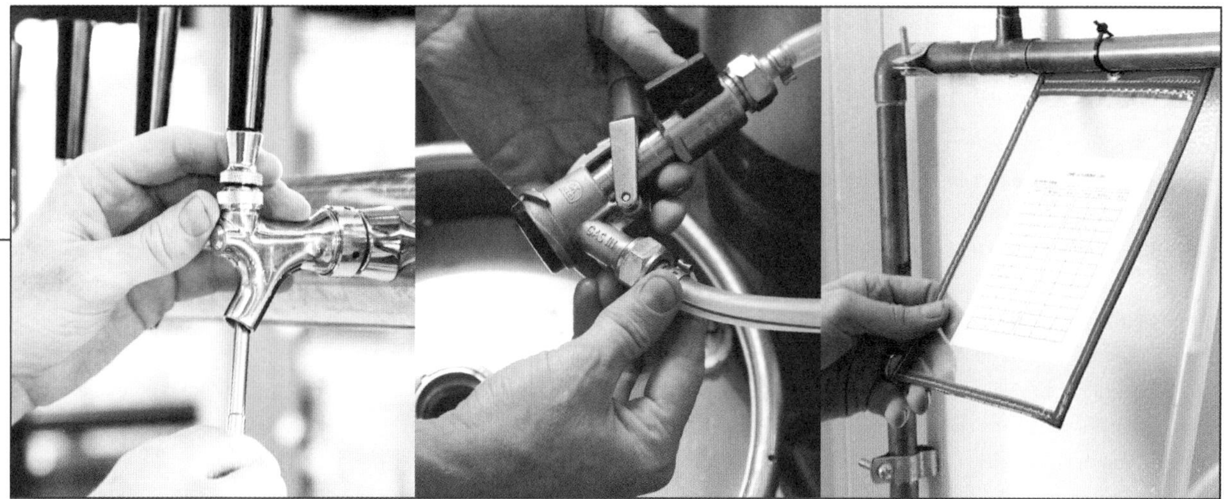

**Figure 7.29.** Faucets and couplers should be inspected visually to ensure that proper line-cleaning frequency and procedure is being followed. Straws can be used to look for soil inside faucets. Line cleaning logs should be maintained.

### Visually Inspecting for Cleanliness

Visually inspecting a draught system for cleanliness (fig. 7.29) is another good indicator of the health of the draught system.

- *Cleaning log.* It is recommended that all draught system cleaners keep a cleaning log that is clearly visible to the retailer, the wholesaler, and the brewer. An example log is shown on page 79. The cleaning log should show the last cleaning having occurred within the last two weeks and an overall two week line-cleaning cycle.
- *Faucets.* Visibly inspect the inside, outside, and vent holes of each faucet. The interior of a faucet can be scraped with the hard edge of a bar straw. Vinegar or butter aromas will indicate a bacterial infection.
- *Couplers.* Visibly inspect the exterior of the coupler. Kegs can be untapped to allow the entire coupler to be inspected. Vinegar or butter aromas will indicate a bacterial infection.
- *FOBs.* Visibly inspect sights glass, vent, and FOB stop. All components, inside and out, should be free of visible build-up. Sight glass should not have any haze and should be completely clear.
- *Jumper lines.* Visibly inspect the flexible tubing in the draught system cooler. The exterior of the tubing should be free of any visible build-up. The tubing should be clear and free of color-staining. Vinyl jumper lines should be replaced every two years.
- *Spill trays.* Visibly inspect the grate and body of the spill tray. The entire spill tray should be free of any visible build-up. Vinegar or butter aromas will indicate a bacterial infection.

Note: Stainless steel is the recommended material for all metal components. Stainless steel will remain cleaner and is a more durable, longer-lasting material.

At this point there are few reliable and realistic ways to test for draught system cleanliness in the field. Because of this, the draught system cleaning and maintenance recommendations from this chapter are designed to be preventive. Once a draught system becomes infected, it becomes extremely difficult—if not impossible—to completely remove. The best defense against bacterial growth is to prevent it with recommended routine hygiene practices. ■

## SUMMARY OF DRAUGHT SYSTEM CLEANING AND SERVICE RECOMMENDATIONS

These guidelines reflect the key actions needed to maintain a clean draught system that will dispense trouble-free, high-quality beer. Before performing these actions, please read the detailed recommendations in this chapter, as they contain many details important to effective and successful cleaning.

**Draught Line Cleaning: Minimum Every Two Weeks (14 days)**

- Clearly posted documentation of line cleaning and servicing records is recommended in all keg coolers. (Visit https://www.brewersassociation.org/educational-publications/draught-beer-line-cleaning-log/ for a printable version of the line cleaning log on page 79).
- Push beer from lines with warm water.
- Clean lines with 2% caustic solution for routine cleaning of well-maintained lines, or with 3% caustic solution for older or more problematic lines. Contact your chemical manufacturer to determine how much chemical is needed to achieve these recommended concentrations. If you use non-caustic-based cleaners, such as acid- or silicate-based cleaners, be sure to use the cleaning concentrations recommended by the manufacturer. For best results, maintain the cleaning solution temperature between 80°F and 110°F during the cleaning process.
- Using an electric pump, caustic solution should be circulated through the lines for a minimum of 15 minutes at a steady flow rate that ideally exceeds the flow rate of the beer. If a pressurized cleaning canister is used (though not recommended), the solution needs to be left standing in the lines for no less than 20 minutes before purging with clean water.
- Disassemble, service, and hand-clean faucets; hand-clean couplers.
- After cleaning, flush lines with cool fresh water until pH matches that of your tap water and no visible debris is being carried from the lines.

**Acid Cleaning: Every Quarter (Three Months)**

- Acid cleanings should be in addition to caustic cleanings, not as a replacement.
- Push beer or caustic cleaner from lines with warm water.
- Clean lines with acid line-cleaner chemical mixed to manufacturer's guidelines. Maintain a solution temperature of 80–110°F.
- Circulate the acid solution through the lines for 15 minutes at a steady flow rate that ideally exceeds the flow rate of the beer. If a pressurized cleaning canister is used (though not recommended), the solution needs to be left standing in the lines for no less than 20 minutes before purging with clean water. After acid cleaning, flush lines with cool fresh water until the pH matches that of your tap water and no visible debris is being carried from the lines.

**Hardware Cleaning: Semi-Annual (Every Six Months)**

- Disassemble, service, and hand-clean all FOB devices (a.k.a. beer savers, foam detectors).
- Disassemble, service, and hand-clean all couplers.

# DRAUGHT BEER LINE CLEANING LOG

ACCOUNT NAME: ______________________________

| DATE | INITALS | CAUSTIC OR ACID, AND BRAND | DATE | INITALS | CAUSTIC OR ACID, AND BRAND | DATE | INITALS | CAUSTIC OR ACID, AND BRAND | DATE | INITALS | CAUSTIC OR ACID, AND BRAND |
|---|---|---|---|---|---|---|---|---|---|---|---|
| | | | | | | | | | | | |
| | | | | | | | | | | | |
| | | | | | | | | | | | |
| | | | | | | | | | | | |
| | | | | | | | | | | | |
| | | | | | | | | | | | |
| | | | | | | | | | | | |
| | | | | | | | | | | | |
| | | | | | | | | | | | |
| | | | | | | | | | | | |
| | | | | | | | | | | | |
| | | | | | | | | | | | |
| | | | | | | | | | | | |
| | | | | | | | | | | | |
| | | | | | | | | | | | |
| | | | | | | | | | | | |
| | | | | | | | | | | | |
| | | | | | | | | | | | |
| | | | | | | | | | | | |

This line-cleaning log can be found at https://www.brewersassociation.org/educational-publications/draught-beer-line-cleaning-log/.

8

# TROUBLESHOOTING

Correctly dispensed draught beer is the result of proper temperature, proper gas pressure and mixture, and a well-maintained draught system. It's easy to take all the variables for granted when beer is pouring well, but improperly pouring beer can be very frustrating and can result in loss of sales. This chapter is intended to provide useful troubleshooting steps anyone can follow to solve draught beer dispensing problems.

The single most common cause of problems encountered in draught dispensing systems is temperature control. The first step in solving any dispensing problem is to confirm that the liquid temperature of the beer in the keg is where it's supposed to be. The next step is to check the temperature of the beer being delivered to the faucet, confirming that the cooling systems used to maintain proper beer line temperature are working properly.

The troubleshooting steps that follow are organized by the type of draught system and how the systems are cooled. Direct-draw systems and long-draw systems cooled by air or glycol each have unique features, which are addressed in this chapter. Other steps addressed include gas pressure and supply, beer supply, and mechanical issues.

**Figure 8.1.** Properly carbonated draught beer that is pouring well should have a head *(left)*. Problems with your draught system can cause undercarbonation *(middle)* and overcarbonation *(right)* when pouring.

**TABLE 8.1.** TROUBLESHOOTING DIRECT-DRAW SYSTEMS

| Problem | Possible Cause | Possible Solution |
|---|---|---|
| **Beer foaming** | Temperature too warm at the faucet (keg box should be 38°F) | Adjust temperature control or call qualified service person |
| | Temperature too cold/frozen beer in lines (should be 38°F) | |
| | Kinked beer line | Change beer line |
| | Wrong beer line length or diameter (should be 4–5 ft. of 3⁄16" ID vinyl tubing; possibly even longer) | |
| | Applied pressure too high | Adjust $CO_2$ regulator to brewer's specification |
| | Applied pressure too low | |
| | Coupler washer defective | Replace coupler washer |
| | Faucet washer defective | Replace faucet washer |
| | System dirty | Clean system or call line cleaning service |
| | $CO_2$ leaks or the draught system is out of $CO_2$ | Check fittings, clamps, shut-offs, and regulators; replace as necessary |
| | Beer foaming in jumper line due to torn or ripped keg valve seal | If seal is ripped/torn, gas enters the liquid flow stream, causing foaming. Replace keg and report defective keg to distributor |
| | Beer foaming in jumper line due to physical obstruction at coupler–valve junction | Remove any physical obstruction or debris (e.g., a piece of a dust cover) that could prevent the coupler from fully engaging and allowing gas to enter the liquid flow |
| | Beer foaming at faucet due to clogged vent hole(s) | Disassemble and clean faucet, or call line cleaning service |
| **No beer at faucet** | Empty $CO_2$ bottle | Replace with full $CO_2$ bottle |
| | Regulator shut-off valve closed | Open shut-off valve |
| | $CO_2$ bottle main valve turned off | Turn on $CO_2$ bottle main valve |
| | Keg empty | Replace with full keg |
| | Coupler not engaged | Tap keg properly and engage coupler |
| | Check ball in coupler one-way valve stuck | Free check ball |
| | Line/faucet dirty | Clean line/faucet |

**TABLE 8.2.** AIR-COOLED SYSTEMS

| Problem | Possible Cause | Possible Solution |
|---|---|---|
| **Beer foaming** | Temperature at faucet too warm (should be 38°F) | Check blower fan's air flow is not obstructed |
| | | Adjust temperature control or call qualified service person |
| | | System designed improperly: too long, wrong size fan, etc. |
| | | Check temperature of beer in keg |
| | Temperature at faucet too cold (should be 38°F) | Adjust temperature control or call qualified service person |
| | Kinked beer line | Change beer line |
| | Wrong size beer line | |
| | Applied pressure too high | Adjust $CO_2$ regulator to brewer's specification |
| | Applied pressure too low | |
| | Wrong dispensing gas (mixed gas blenders recommended) | Change to mixed gas blender and use target pressure |
| | Coupler washer defective | Replace coupler washer |
| | Faucet washer defective | Replace faucet washer |
| | System dirty | Clean system or call line cleaning service |
| | Beer foaming in jumper line due to torn or ripped keg valve seal | If seal is ripped/torn, gas enters the liquid flow stream, causing foaming. Replace keg and report defective keg to distributor |
| | Beer foaming in jumper line due to physical obstruction at coupler–valve junction | Remove any physical obstruction or debris (e.g., a piece of a dust cover) that could prevent the coupler from fully engaging and allowing gas to enter the liquid flow |
| | Beer foaming at faucet due to clogged vent hole(s) | Disassemble and clean faucet, or call line cleaning service |
| **No beer at faucet** | Empty $CO_2$ bottle, $N_2$ bottle, or mixed gas bottle | Replace with appropriate full gas bottle |
| | Regulator shut-off valve closed | Open shut-off valve |
| | Gas bottle main valve turned off | Turn on gas bottle main valve |
| | Keg empty | Replace with full keg |
| | Coupler not engaged | Tap keg properly and engage coupler |
| | Check ball in coupler one-way valve stuck | Free check ball |
| | Line/faucet dirty | Clean line/faucet |

**Note:** For air-cooled systems, the maximum recommended distance for a double-duct system is 25 ft. (tube side by side) and for a single-duct system it is 15 ft. (tube within a tube).

**TABLE 8.3.** GLYCOL-CHILLED SYSTEMS

| Problem | Possible Cause | Possible Solution |
|---|---|---|
| **Beer foaming** | Temperature at faucet too warm or too cold (should be 38°F) | Check glycol chillers for proper operation; adjust glycol bath temperature if too warm or too cold (most systems are designed to operate between 28°F and 34°F; check unit manufacturer's specs) |
| | | Adjust temperature control or call qualified service person |
| | Wrong dispensing gas (glycol systems usually require a mixed gas blender) | Change to mixed gas blender and use target pressure |
| | Glycol pump functioning (check return line) | Call qualified service person to adjust glycol chiller temperature or operation |
| | Gas regulators incorrectly set | Contact installer |
| | Applied pressure too low | Adjust $CO_2$ regulator to brewer's specification |
| | Applied pressure too high | |
| | Coupler washer defective | Replace coupler washer |
| | Faucet washer defective | Replace faucet washer |
| | System dirty | Clean system or call line cleaning service |
| | Glycol power pack failure; check condenser, glycol concentration | Call qualified service person to clean clogged condenser fins, check glycol strength, and service glycol chiller |
| | Beer foaming in jumper line due to torn or ripped keg valve seal | If seal is ripped/torn, gas enters the liquid flow stream causing foaming. Replace keg and report defective keg to distributor |
| | Beer foaming in jumper line due to physical obstruction at coupler–valve junction | Remove any physical obstruction or debris (e.g., a piece of a dust cover) that could prevent the coupler from fully engaging and allowing gas to enter the liquid flow |
| | Beer foaming at faucet due to clogged vent hole(s) | Disassemble and clean faucet, or call line cleaning service |
| **No beer at faucet** | Empty $CO_2$ source, $N_2$ source, or mixed gas bottle | Replace with appropriate full gas bottle; refill bulk $CO_2$ or $N_2$ tank; check nitrogen generator |
| | Regulator shut-off valve closed | Open shut-off valve |
| | Gas bottle or bulk tank main valve turned off | Turn on gas bottle or tank main valve |
| | Keg empty | Replace with full keg |
| | Coupler not engaged | Tap keg properly and engage coupler |
| | Check ball in coupler one-way valve stuck | Free check ball |
| | Line/faucet obstructed | Clear line/faucet of obstruction by cleaning; if frozen, allow lines to thaw |
| | FOB needs reset | Reset FOB |
| | Pneumatic beer pump(s) failure | Check gas supply to pump(s); check pump diverter setting |

**Note:** A glycol system is designed to maintain liquid beer temperature from the cooler to the dispensing point.

## OFF-FLAVORS IN DRAUGHT BEER

The purpose of this manual is to explain how to maintain the correct flavor of your draught beer. When fresh and properly dispensed, draught beer will taste the way the brewer intended—clean, flavorful, and enjoyable. Draught beer is susceptible to damage from a host of factors, such as age, heat, and air. But the number one preventable factor affecting draught beer flavor and aroma is poor hygiene.

Improper cleaning of draught system lines and components—from the coupler in the cooler to the faucet at the bar—can lead to significant changes in beer flavor, all of them unwelcome. Over time, poor beer line hygiene will inevitably result in loss of sales due to customer dissatisfaction, and necessitate replacing beer lines at great expense. Staying ahead of these potentially costly outcomes is key to serving great-tasting draught beer.

Table 8.4 on page 86 lists the most common off-flavors that occur due to post-brewery unhygienic conditions and the mishandling of draught beer. While they are not health risks, beer-spoiling bacteria will ruin a beer's flavor and aroma. Such bacterial infections in draught systems are often difficult, if not impossible, to completely remove. By following the guidelines outlined in this manual the occurrence of these off-flavors can be prevented. ■

**TABLE 8.4.** COMMON CAUSES OF OFF-FLAVORS IN BEER

| Off-Flavor | Off-Flavor Description | Bacteria | Likely Causes | How to Prevent and Resolve |
|---|---|---|---|---|
| **Diacetyl** | Buttery, buttered popcorn, butterscotch, or caramel; can have a slick or milky mouthfeel at high levels | Anaerobic bacteria: *Pediococcus* (most likely), *Lactobacillus* (less likely) | Diacetyl is the most common off-flavor associated with dirty draught systems. *Pediococcus* and *Lactobacillus* arise due to unhygienic conditions in draught beer systems. These bacteria are most likely to develop when:<br>• the cleaning frequency extends beyond a two-week cycle<br>• an electric recirculating line-cleaning pump is not regularly used<br>• associated draught system equipment is not properly disassembled, serviced, and hand-cleaned at the recommended intervals<br>• improper chemicals or low chemical concentrations are used<br>• beer lines are older than their recommended age<br>• kegs in series are not completely emptied on a weekly basis<br>• ineffective line cleaning procedures are used | Completely removing a bacterial infection from a beer line can be very difficult, if not impossible. Even after cleaning, these bacteria may remain in the beer line and keg at initially undetectable levels. However, in a short time, these anaerobic bacteria will resurface as an overpowering infection. The goal is to completely rid the system of any traces of bacteria so the off-flavors never return.<br>Prior to cleaning, begin by replacing infected hardware and beer lines wherever possible, and always replace any kegs that have been tapped into an infected system. Follow the step-by-step electric recirculating pump cleaning procedures in chapter 7, rotating between caustic and acid cycles to maximize your chances of removal |
| **Lactic acid** | Sour, sour milk; acidic (note that the bacterial load would have to be very large to pick up the acidic flavor) | Anaerobic bacteria: *Lactobacillus* (most likely), *Pediococcus* (less likely) | | |
| **Acetic acid** | Sour, vinegar | Aerobic bacteria *Acetobacter* | *Acetobacter* growth usually begins in or on dirty drains, spill trays, bar tops, or used bar rags and will eventually spread to the beer dispensing faucets. Serving staff submerging a faucet into a beer will increase the growth rate of these bacteria.<br>The leading cause of *Acetobacter* infection comes from faucets not being completely disassembled and hand-detailed on a two-week cycle. | Serving staff should be thoroughly trained on proper serving techniques (see chapter 6).<br>Beer faucets should be completely disassembled and hand-detailed using caustic chemicals every two weeks.<br>Stainless steel is the best material for preventing bacterial buildup on faucets |
| **Oxidation** | Papery, cardboard, fruity, bready, vinous, vegetal<br>These are only a few descriptors. Oxidation is a very broad term and different ingredients will take on different oxidative properties | Not applicable.<br>Oxidation in beer is a reaction that occurs when a beer is exposed to oxygen | Oxidation occurs due to time, temperature, or direct exposure to oxygen. All beers have an expiration date. This is the date by which point a brewery feels the beer has taken on significant oxidative properties, and that the beer no longer represents the brewery-intended flavor.<br>A beer's expiration date can easily be shortened by exposure to warm temperatures. Draught beer should be kept cold (below 50°F) at all times to maximize its freshness. The longer a beer is kept warm and/or the higher the temperature, the faster the beer will oxidize. If a beer ever rises above 80°F, for any amount of time, the beer is likely ruined.<br>In draught beers, oxidation can happen with the use of an air compressor (chapter 1). If an air compressor is used to dispense draught beer, oxygen will be forced into the keg and oxidize a beer within 24 hours.<br>Porous tubing material will allow oxygen to leach through to the beer, especially if the beer sits in the line for extended lengths of time between pours | Take note of brewery recommended best-by and consume-by dates and temperature specifications. Monitor conditions to ensure your beer stays within brewery recommended guidelines.<br>Ensure any kegs in series have been completely emptied (series kegs should be completely emptied and replaced once per week).<br>Never use compressed air in direct contact with draught beer.<br>Use barrier and stainless steel tubing whenever possible (see chapter 4) |

# APPENDIX A

## ISBT GUIDELINES FOR BEVERAGE GRADE CARBON DIOXIDE

The International Society of Beverage Technologists (ISBT) publishes quality guidelines relating to the quality and purity of $CO_2$ used in beverages. Table A.1 reproduces the ISBT's recommended limits for parameters commonly tested for in beverage grade $CO_2$. ■

**TABLE A.1.** ISBT QUALITY GUIDELINES FOR BEVERAGE GRADE $CO_2$

| Parameter | ISBT limit |
|---|---|
| Purity | Min. 99.9% |
| Moisture | Max. 20 ppm |
| Oxygen | Max. 30 ppm |
| Carbon monoxide | Max. 10 ppm |
| Ammonia | Max. 2.5 ppm |
| Nitric oxide | Max. 2.5 ppm |
| Nitrogen dioxide | Max. 2.5 ppm |
| Nonvolatile residue | Max. (w/w) 10 ppm |
| Nonvolatile organic residue | Max. (w/w) 5 ppm |
| Phosphine | Max. 0.3 ppm |
| Total volatile hydrocarbons | Max. 50 ppm |
| Acetaldehyde | Max. 0.2 ppm |
| Aromatic hydrocarbon | Max. 20 ppb |
| Total sulfur content (as S) | Max. 0.1 ppm |
| Sulfur dioxide | Max. 1 ppm |
| Odor of solid $CO_2$ | No foreign odor |
| Appearance in water | No color or turbidity |
| Odor and taste in water | No foreign taste or odor |

**Note:** Specified concentrations are volume per volume (v/v) unless otherwise noted.
Max., maximum; min., minimum; ppb, parts per billion; ppm, parts per million; w/w, weight per weight.

# APPENDIX B

## $CO_2$ EQUILIBRIUM GAUGE PRESSURE REFERENCE CHART

**TABLE B.1.** DETERMINATION OF PURE $CO_2$ EQUILIBRIUM GAUGE PRESSURE (PSIG) FOR GIVEN VOLUMES OF $CO_2$ AND TEMPERATURE

| | Volumes of $CO_2$ | | | | | | | | | | |
|---|---|---|---|---|---|---|---|---|---|---|---|
| **Temp. (°F)** | **2.1** | **2.2** | **2.3** | **2.4** | **2.5** | **2.6** | **2.7** | **2.8** | **2.9** | **3.0** | **3.1** |
| **33** | 5.0 | 6.0 | 6.9 | 7.9 | 8.8 | 9.8 | 10.7 | 11.7 | 12.6 | 13.6 | 14.5 |
| **34** | 5.2 | 6.2 | 7.2 | 8.1 | 9.1 | 10.1 | 11.1 | 12.0 | 13.0 | 14.0 | 15.0 |
| **35** | 5.6 | 6.6 | 7.6 | 8.6 | 9.7 | 10.7 | 11.7 | 12.7 | 13.7 | 14.8 | 15.8 |
| **36** | 6.1 | 7.1 | 8.2 | 9.2 | 10.2 | 11.3 | 12.3 | 13.4 | 14.4 | 15.5 | 16.5 |
| **37** | 6.6 | 7.6 | 8.7 | 9.8 | 10.8 | 11.9 | 12.9 | 14.0 | 15.1 | 16.1 | 17.2 |
| **38** | 7.0 | 8.1 | 9.2 | 10.3 | 11.3 | 12.4 | 13.5 | 14.5 | 15.6 | 16.7 | 17.8 |
| **39** | 7.6 | 8.7 | 9.8 | 10.8 | 11.9 | 13.0 | 14.1 | 15.2 | 16.3 | 17.4 | 18.5 |
| **40** | 8.0 | 9.1 | 10.2 | 11.3 | 12.4 | 13.5 | 14.6 | 15.7 | 16.8 | 17.9 | 19.0 |
| **41** | 8.3 | 9.4 | 10.6 | 11.7 | 12.8 | 13.9 | 15.1 | 16.2 | 17.3 | 18.4 | 19.5 |
| **42** | 8.8 | 9.9 | 11.0 | 12.2 | 13.3 | 14.4 | 15.6 | 16.7 | 17.8 | 19.0 | 20.1 |

**Source:** Data from *Methods of Analysis*, 5th ed., (Milwaukee, WI: American Society of Brewing Chemists, 1949).

**Notes:** Values assume sea-level altitude, beer specific gravity of 1.015, and beer alcohol content at 3.8% ABW or 4.8% ABV. Values shown are in psig, or gauge pressure.

It is important to remember that carbonation is proportional to absolute pressure, not gauge pressure. Atmospheric pressure drops as elevation goes up. Therefore, the gauge pressure needed to achieve proper carbonation at elevations above sea level must be increased. Add 1 psig for every 2000 ft. above sea level. For example, a retailer at sea level would use 11.3 psig to maintain 2.5 volumes $CO_2$ in beer served at 38°F. That same retailer at 4000 ft. above sea level would need 13.3 psig to maintain 2.5 volumes $CO_2$.

### FIGURING IDEAL GAUGE PRESSURE WHEN CARBONATION LEVEL IS NOT KNOWN

The ideal gauge pressure for a beer is the pressure at which $CO_2$ is not diffusing from beer into the head space and excess $CO_2$ is not absorbing in the beer. If you know the carbonation level of your beer, you can determine the ideal gauge pressure for pure (100%) $CO_2$ using table B.1.

If you do not know the carbonation level in your beer, you can estimate it using the following procedure:

1. Set the regulator pressure to 5 psi.
2. Tap a fresh keg. Make sure the keg has been in the cooler long enough to be at the cooler temperature.
3. Pour a small amount of beer through the faucet.
4. Observe the beer in the draught line directly above the keg coupler (with a flashlight if necessary), inspecting for bubbles rising up from the beer in the keg.
5. If bubbles are present, raise the regulator pressure by 1 psi.
6. Repeat steps 3–5 until no bubbles are present.
7. Check the keg temperature 24 hours after setting the initial gauge pressure to assure temperature stability, and to reset the gauge pressure as needed due to a change in keg temperature.

The above procedure achieves the lowest pressure at which the gas in the beer is not escaping. This is your ideal gauge pressure.

### CONVERTING VOLUMES OF $CO_2$ TO GRAMS PER LITER

In the United States, carbonation is expressed in units of "volumes of $CO_2$." What this means is that one keg of beer carbonated to 2.5 volumes of $CO_2$ contains 2.5 keg-volumes of $CO_2$ compressed and dissolved into the beer. In other countries, carbonation is usually expressed in units of grams per liter, meaning the amount of $CO_2$ in grams dissolved in one liter of beer. To convert between volumes of $CO_2$ and grams per liter, the quick and easy answer is 2 g/L equals 1 volume of $CO_2$.

However, 2 g/L = 1 vol. $CO_2$ is not exactly correct. There are several alternative values and methods to calculate the conversion, as described below.

A first approximation can be found by assuming that $CO_2$ has a molar mass of 44 grams per mole (g/mol) and that one mole of a gas at standard temperature and pressure (STP) conditions (i.e., 0°C, 1 atm) occupies a volume of 22.4 liters. Finding the conversion factor to go from g/L to volumes $CO_2$ is as follows:

$$\frac{1\text{g } CO_2}{1\text{L beer}} \times \frac{1\text{mol } CO_2}{44\text{g } CO_2} \times \frac{22.4\text{L}}{1\text{mol } CO_2} = \frac{22.4}{44} = 0.509$$

The reciprocal of this value gives you the conversion factor for converting from volumes of $CO_2$ to g/L:

$$\frac{1}{0.509} = 1.965$$

For a slightly more accurate answer we can use the value of 44.01 g/mol for $CO_2$ and 22.426 L/mol for the STP volume of $CO_2$ gas. We can also take account of the fact that $CO_2$ does not behave strictly in accordance with the ideal gas law and has a compressibility factor ($Z$) of 0.99952 under STP conditions. Using these values we get 1.966 instead of 1.965. Not much difference there, but perhaps a better sense of accuracy.

Another tool is the National Institute of Standards and Technology Standard Reference Database 23.[1] The 2010 version of this database gives a value for the density of $CO_2$ under STP conditions of 1.9768 g/L. This may be accepted as the most accurate value to use as a conversion factor and it is the one to use if doing an exact analysis.

So, to quickly convert volumes of $CO_2$ to grams per liter in your head, "2" is an acceptable conversion factor. In cases where you want to have more accuracy, you can use 1.9768 or whatever rounded-off value you feel comfortable with. ■

[1] NIST Standard Reference Database 23: Fluid Thermodynamic and Transport Properties Database (REFPROP) (Version 9.0; published November 1, 2010), https://www.nist.gov/srd.

# APPENDIX C

## CARBONATION, BLENDED GAS, GAS LAWS, AND PARTIAL PRESSURES

### CARBONATION

In general, the amount of carbonation in beer depends primarily on the pressure of $CO_2$ applied to the keg of beer being dispensed, and the temperature of the beer. In reality, many other factors can also affect carbonation levels, including the blended proportion of $CO_2$, alcohol content, and specific gravity. Knowing a bit about these factors can help you fine-tune your draught dispensing system to achieve the perfect pour for every brand dispensed.

### DEFINING MIXED GASES

For the purposes of this manual, as a convention in discussions involving mixed gas, the proportion of $CO_2$ will always be shown first, followed by the proportion of $N_2$.

*Temperature.* In general, gas is less soluble in liquid as the temperature rises. This seems obvious—a nicely chilled keg of beer dispenses easily, while that same keg of beer dispenses as foam if it gets warm.

*Proportion of $CO_2$ in blended gas.* The proportion of $CO_2$ in the gas blend is directly related to the pressure of the $CO_2$ in the head space in the keg. Two different gas laws—Dalton's law of partial pressure and Henry's law—can help us make sense of what's going on. This is most easily described by example, along with a little math. Consider a situation in which a keg of beer is dispensed using gas at 20 psig. If pure $CO_2$ is used to dispense beer, then all of the pressure on that keg is due to $CO_2$. But what if the gas being used is a blend of 75% $CO_2$ and 25% $N_2$? In this case, Dalton's law can help us figure out what's going on. Dalton's law of partial pressure says that *the total pressure exerted* *by a gaseous mixture is equal to the sum of the partial pressures of each individual component in the mixture.* This means the partial pressure of $CO_2$ is equal to the proportion of $CO_2$ in the gas, in this case 75%, times the total absolute pressure of the blended gas, in this case 34.7 psia (20 psig + 14.7 psi atmospheric pressure = 34.7 psia). In this case, the partial pressure of $CO_2$ is:

$$0.75 \times 34.7 \text{ psia} = 26.0 \text{ psi}$$

To relate this $CO_2$ partial pressure in terms of applied gauge pressure, we simply take away the atmospheric pressure:

$$26.0 \text{ psi} - 14.7 \text{ psi atmospheric} = 11.3 \text{ psig}$$

So, in this example using a 75%/25% gas blend, the carbonation of the beer will be proportional to 11.3 psig of $CO_2$, *not* 20 psig $CO_2$. It is important to note this calculation must be done using absolute pressure, then converted to gauge pressure. (If you used the 20 psig value rather than 34.7 psia, 75% of that value would result in 15 psig as the partial pressure of $CO_2$ in this scenario, which is not correct.) Consulting table B.1 on page 89 and assuming a temperature of 38°F and 11.3 psi $CO_2$ pressure, the carbonation level in this example would be 2.5 volumes (rather than 2.8–2.9 volumes, which would be the 15 psi result if you had incorrectly used gauge pressure).

*Alcohol Content and Specific Gravity.* Most of the liquid in beer is water. The standard carbonation table (table B.1) is based on beer containing 4.8% alcohol by volume (ABV), so approximately 95% of the liquid is water. As it turns out, $CO_2$ is more soluble in ethanol than it is in water. Therefore, the solubility of $CO_2$ in the beer increases as the ABV increases. The degree to which ABV affects solubility in different beers is hard to calculate, however, due to the opposing effects of a beer's density on $CO_2$ solubility.

Specific gravity, or the density of the beer, is affected by other compounds in solution, such as carbohydrates and proteins that provide mouthfeel, body, color, and flavor. As the density of beer increases, there is effectively less liquid available into which $CO_2$ can dissolve. While not always the case, high ABV beers tend to have a higher specific gravity. Therefore, a high ABV beer may have an increased $CO_2$ solubility from the alcohol content, but that effect is outweighed by the opposing decrease in solubility due to the beer's greater density from carbohydrates, proteins, and other compounds within the beer.

### The Dispensing Gas Blend Affects Carbonation

Henry's law says that *the solubility of a gas in a liquid is directly proportional to the partial pressure of the gas above the liquid.* This turns out to be really useful when dispensing beer in systems where more than 12–15 psi of dispensing pressure is needed to move beer to the taps, such as long-draw systems.

The partial pressure of a gas within a blend can be calculated by multiplying the total pressure of the gas blend (in psia, not psig) times the proportion of that gas in the blend. Let's consider a couple of scenarios in which draught beer is (1) dispensed using a 70%/30% gas blend, and (2) dispensed using 100% $CO_2$. In both scenarios, let's assume the dispensing temperature is 39°F, and that the system has been designed and balanced to dispense beer at an operating pressure of 20 psig, or 34.7 psia (i.e., 20 + 14.7).

*Scenario 1: Dispensing with blended gas at 70%/30%.* The carbonation in the beer will depend on the partial pressure of $CO_2$, which equals the absolute pressure of the gas blend times the proportion of $CO_2$:

$$\text{total dispensing pressure} \times \text{proportion } CO_2 \text{ in blend} = \text{partial pressure } CO_2$$

$$34.7 \text{ psi} \times 0.70 = 24.3 \text{ psi}$$

To find the gauge pressure for the $CO_2$ partial pressure we must account for atmospheric pressure, which is 14.7 psi at sea level.

$$\text{partial pressure } CO_2 - \text{atmospheric pressure} = \text{applied partial pressure } CO_2$$

$$24.3 \text{ psia} - 14.7 \text{ psi} = 9.6 \text{ psig}$$

An applied partial pressure of 9.6 psig for $CO_2$ at 39°F would result in about 2.3 volumes of $CO_2$ in beer. This carbonation level is a bit lower than typical values of 2.5–2.7 volumes found in most beer brands.

*Scenario 2: Dispensing with 100% $CO_2$.* The carbonation in the beer will depend on the partial pressure of $CO_2$, which in this case is easily derived because we are using 100% $CO_2$:

$$\text{total dispensing pressure} \times \text{proportion } CO_2 \text{ in blend} = \text{partial pressure } CO_2$$

$$34.7 \text{ psia} \times 1.0 = 34.7 \text{ psi}$$

To find the gauge pressure for $CO_2$ partial pressure we must account for atmospheric pressure, which is 14.7 psi at sea level:

$$\text{partial pressure } CO_2 - \text{atmospheric pressure} = \text{applied partial pressure } CO_2$$

$$34.7 \text{ psi} - 14.7 \text{ psi} = 20 \text{ psig}$$

An applied partial pressure of 20 psig for $CO_2$ at 39°F would result in about 3.25 volumes of $CO_2$ in the beer. This carbonation level is considerably higher than typical values of 2.5–2.7 volumes.

From these two examples, we can see that, at the operating parameters of the system in question, pure $CO_2$ would result in carbonation levels that are too high, whereas the 70%/30% blend we chose would result in carbonation levels that are a bit too low. So, is there a way to use Henry's law to figure out the exact blend for our draught system? And, looking at this another way, is there a way to use this math to figure out the ideal gauge pressure to use, given a certain blend of gas?

As it turns out, there are tools available online to do both of these tasks with a great degree of accuracy. There are also some relatively straightforward calculations that do the same things very quickly, which we will go on to show here. The following equation is very useful for relating gauge pressure, absolute pressure, and proportion of $CO_2$ in a blend:

$$c = \frac{b + 14.7}{a + 14.7}$$

where $a$ is the gauge pressure of the blended gas, $b$ is the ideal gauge pressure of pure $CO_2$ (refer to table B.1 in appendix B), $c$ is the proportion of $CO_2$ in the blended gas, and atmospheric pressure is assumed to be 14.7 psi (i.e., sea level).

## CALCULATING GAS BLENDS AND PRESSURES

### Determining the Ideal $CO_2$ / $N_2$ Blend

Determining the ideal mix of $CO_2$ and $N_2$ in a gas blend for a given draught dispensing system can be done using the equation we introduced at the end of the previous section.

Let's go back to our example above, in which a draught system was designed to operate at 39°F and 20 psig. Let's also assume that the beers being poured are carbonated to 2.5 volumes of $CO_2$. From table B.1 on page 89, we see that a beer at 2.5 volumes of $CO_2$ at 39°F has an equilibrium pressure of 11.9 psi of $CO_2$. Given that

$$c = \frac{b + 14.7}{a + 14.7}$$

where $a$ is the gauge pressure of the blended gas, $b$ is the ideal gauge pressure of pure $CO_2$, and $c$ is the proportion of $CO_2$ in the blended gas, we now know that $a$ = 20 psi and $b$ = 11.9 psi. Plugging in the values:

$$c = \frac{11.9 + 14.7}{20 + 14.7}$$

$$= 26.6/34.7$$

$$= 0.767, \text{ or } 76.7\%$$

So, once we round up 76.7% to 77%, we find the ideal blend is 77% $CO_2$ and 23% $N_2$.

What if we wanted to also dispense beers with 2.7 volumes of $CO_2$ in this same retail establishment? From table B.1, we see that a beer at 2.7 volumes of $CO_2$ at 39°F has an equilibrium pressure of 14.1 psi of $CO_2$. In this case, $a$ = 20 psi and $b$ = 14.1 psi, and we can again solve for $c$, the proportion of $CO_2$:

$$c = \frac{14.1 + 14.7}{20 + 14.7}$$

$$= 28.8/34.7$$

$$= 0.83, \text{ or } 83\%$$

In this case, a gas blender with more than one blend of mixed gas would be very helpful. You would use the 77% $CO_2$ to dispense beers with 2.5 volumes of carbonation, and the 83% blend to dispense beers with 2.7 volumes of carbonation.

### Determining the Correct Pressure for a Fixed $CO_2$ / $N_2$ Blend

What if, in the above examples, we only had access to one blend of gas? Could we adjust the pressure a bit to achieve more than one level of carbonation, and still dispense beer in the same draught system? Well, maybe. This is very similar to the procedure outlined on page 39 in chapter 4 of this manual. Let's go back to our example above, in which a draught system is designed to operate at 39°F and 20 psig. We want to dispense beers carbonated to both 2.5 and 2.7 volumes of $CO_2$, but we only have a single-mix blender.

From the previous section, we know that the 77% $CO_2$ blend is correct for the 2.5 volume beers. What pressure would we have to use to correctly dispense beers with 2.7 volumes of $CO_2$ using this 77% blend? Look again at the equation:

$$c = \frac{b + 14.7}{a + 14.7}$$

where $a$ is the gauge pressure of the blended gas, $b$ is the ideal gauge pressure of pure $CO_2$, and $c$ is the proportion of $CO_2$ in the blended gas. In this case, $a$ is our unknown, so we must rearrange the equation to solve for $a$:

$$c = \frac{b + 14.7}{a + 14.7}$$

Multiply both sides by ($a$ + 14.7)

$$c(a + 14.7) = b + 14.7$$

Divide both sides by $c$

$$a + 14.7 = \frac{b + 14.7}{c}$$

Minus 14.7 to isolate $a$

$$a = \left(\frac{b + 14.7}{c}\right) - 14.7$$

Now we have the equation to solve for $a$, and we know that $b = 14.1$ and $c = 0.77$, we can calculate the gauge pressure:

$$a = \left(\frac{b + 14.7}{c}\right) - 14.7$$

$$= (28.8/0.77) - 14.7$$

$$= 37.4 - 14.7$$

$$a = 22.7 \text{ psi}$$

So, in theory, if we increase the dispensing pressure from 20 psi to 22.7 psi on those kegs of beer carbonated to 2.7 volumes of $CO_2$, we could use the same 77% $CO_2$ blend to dispense them and maintain proper carbonation. This may or may not work in reality. The beer might pour too fast at the bar, creating turbulence within the glassware; but, the beer may have an acceptable pour with the right amount of carbonation. Experimentation at the bar will reveal if the pressure increase worked, or if an additional blend is needed. ■

# APPENDIX D
## NOTES ON SERVING CASK ALE

Cask ale, sometimes called cask-conditioned beer or "real ale," is draught beer dispensed and served in a traditional method. Cask ale is generally served at warmer temperatures than regularly carbonated draught beer, and without an extraneous propellant. The result is a beer with different presentation, flavor, and aroma, quite unlike that from the same beer force carbonated and dispensed with $CO_2$ or mixed gas applied pressure.

In this appendix, we focus on a few particulars of dispensing cask ale that represent basic knowledge and best practices. The production of cask ale is an art unto itself, sometimes referred to as cellarmanship, the details of which are well beyond the scope of this manual.

### TEMPERATURE

Cask ale is typically conditioned and dispensed at 45–55°F, unlike the colder 36–38°F range for regularly carbonated draught beer. The temperature is warm enough to allow the beer within the cask to develop its own natural carbonation due to the presence of living yeast. The higher temperature also means that $CO_2$ is not as soluble in the beer, and the result is a beer that is far less carbonated.

### CARBONATION

Because cask ale is handled at warmer temperatures, and since $CO_2$ is less soluble at warmer temperatures, cask ale contains much lower levels of carbonation than regular draught beer. Cask beer typically contains 0.9–1.2 volumes of $CO_2$, far less than the 2.5–2.7 volumes typical of force carbonated draught beer.

The carbonation in cask ale arises from natural secondary fermentation within the cask, rather than from force carbonation at the brewery. The relatively warmer cellaring temperatures allow this fermentation to occur after the cask leaves the brewery.

## DISPENSING CASK ALE

Cask ale is normally dispensed from a cask located relatively close to the bar, or even on the bar or back bar. Most modern casks are metal, although a few wooden varieties are sometimes still found. Most casks contain two openings that are filled with wooden or plastic plugs called shives (for letting gas in) and keystones (for tapping and removing beer). The cask is placed on its side with the shive up and the keystone down. A spile is used to vent the cask through the shive. There are two kinds of spiles available: soft spiles, which are porous, and hard spiles, which are made of denser, harder wood. The soft spile is used initially in order to allow gas to escape the cask during fermentation. Once this process is complete, the soft spile is replaced with a hard spile in order to prevent gas from exiting the cask. Cask ale is dispensed without top pressure, meaning that it either pours from the cask through a faucet-like tap directly into the glass using gravity, or the beer is pumped a short distance using a pump called a beer engine (fig. D.1).

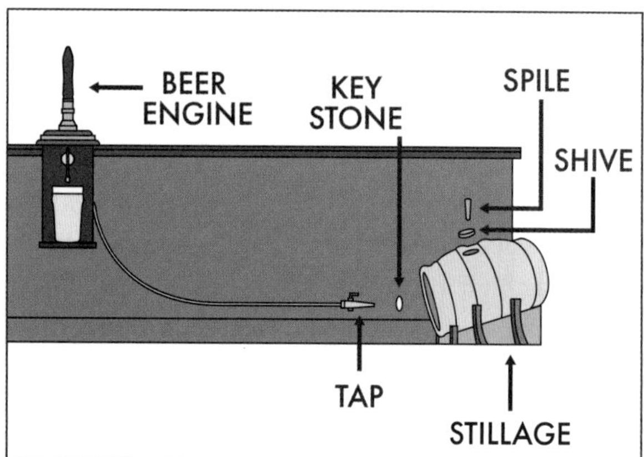


**Figure D.1.** Typical configuration for dispensing cask ale using a beer engine.

The cask should be allowed to settle for several hours, even up to a day, before serving. This process, called stillaging, allows the yeast in the cask to settle to the bottom and the beer to pour clear.

While pouring a cask, gas is allowed to enter the cask being emptied in order to prevent a vacuum from forming. Busy bars that empty a cask in one to three days will sometimes allow air to enter the cask. Another option is to use $CO_2$ at atmospheric pressure to fill the head space. A device called a "cask breather" can be used to top-off the head space as the beer is dispensed, which prevents the ingress of air and potential beer spoilers (fig. D.2). Carbon dioxide is preferable to air in terms of preserving the beer, but there is some disagreement about whether this practice is "proper" because it is not traditional. This manual is not the forum for that discussion.

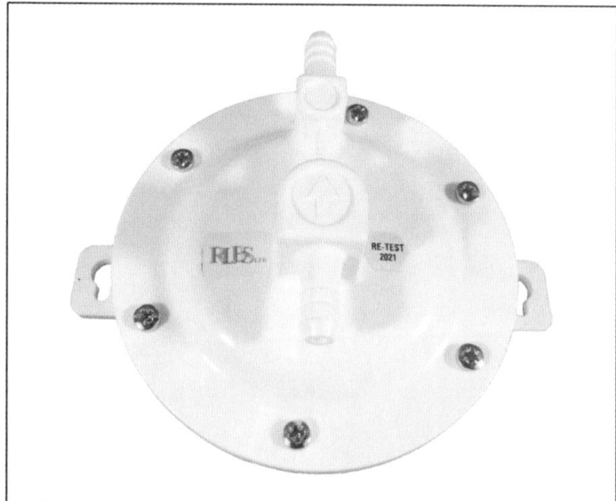

**Figure D.2.** Cask breather.

Cask ale dispensed directly from a cask using a gravity dispense tap will usually have very low amounts of foam in the glass (fig. D.3). Cask ale dispensed from a beer engine may be poured through a fitting called a sparkler that serves to create foam from the very low level of carbonation present.

**Figure D.3.** Dispensing cask ale using a gravity dispense tap.

Photo © The Brewtography Project

### Beer Engines

Beer engines dispense cask beer (fig. D.4.). Pulling the handle actuates a piston or chamber of the engine and pumps beer from the cask to the customer's glass. Beer engines can be clamp-on or built into a bar. Some breweries that make cask ales will require a sparkler (perforated disk) that attaches to the end of the pouring spout.

**Figure D.4.** Dispensing cask ale using a beer engine.

## CASK ALE BEST PRACTICES

Pouring cask ale from a swan neck beer engine faucet is the only instance when the faucet should come into contact with the inside of a beer glass. Due to the unique nature of this beer dispensing system, a list of guidelines must be followed to ensure proper sanitation and high product quality.

1. At the start of the day, discard the first pull of beer to empty the beer engine cylinder of beer that has been sitting overnight.
2. Always use a beer-clean glass for every serving of cask ale dispensed from a beer engine. This should be the case when pouring any draught beer, but even more so with cask ale due to the potential to transfer germs from one glass to another.
3. The closing bartender should do one final clean of the cask faucet, drip tray, and the surface of the entire cask pump when the bar closes. This cleaning should be done with restaurant/bar sanitizer approved by your local and state health code. If the cask faucet uses a sparkler, the sparkler should be removed and soaked overnight in the same sanitizer at a soaking concentration listed by the manufacturer.
4. The opening bartender should wipe the cask faucet with a clean towel wetted with fresh water before the first cask beer is pulled to ensure any residual sanitizer from the previous night is removed. If the cask pump is fitted with a sparkler, thoroughly rinse the sparkler under fresh water before attaching it to the cask faucet.
5. After the cask has been emptied, remove the shive and rinse the inside of cask thoroughly with warm water as soon as possible.

### Cask System Hygiene

Cleanliness is paramount in the handling of cask ale. Unlike kegged draught beer, items are being inserted into beer such as taps, spiles, and ale extractors. These all give an opportunity for bacteria to be introduced.

- Run clean, warm water through the beer line and beer engine between every cask.
- Perform regular beer line cleaning every 14 days, just like regular draught beer lines.
  - Be sure to check with the manufacturer of the beer engine to ensure the cleaning solution concentration is compatible with the piston, so as not to damage it.
  - Using the hand pump, draw the chemical solution through the beer line until beer engine is filled with chemical solution. Allow for 20 minutes contact time.
  - Purge the system of the chemical solution by drawing through cool water. Ensure that all of the chemical is removed by testing the pH of the rinse water.

### Pouring Cask Ale with a Head

While some customers may ask their beer be "filled to the rim," brewers prefer beer poured with about a one-inch collar of foam, which is the beer's "head." The importance of a one-inch foam collar should not be underestimated. The purpose of a proper head on any cask ale is the same as a draught beer; the head helps to deliver the total sensory experience:

- a good pour has visual appeal
- the beer releases more aromatic volatiles
- the palate-cleansing effects of carbonation are enhanced
- the beer presents a better overall textural and sensorial experience to the consumer

Well-prepared cask ale will easily allow for one inch of head or more if a sparkler is fitted on the end of the faucet. Without the sparkler device, a full one-inch collar of foam may be difficult to achieve. The bar or restaurant manager should consult the brewer to discuss how their particular beer is intended to be served. ■

# DRAUGHT BEER GLOSSARY

**Absolute pressure** – Absolute pressure is the total pressure on the beer, and is the sum of atmospheric pressure plus any additional applied pressure from the dispensing gas.

**Acid cleaner** – Although several blends of acid cleaners are recommended to assist in beer stone and water stone removal, some acids react with system components. Phosphoric acid-based blends are the only ones safe on all materials.

**Atmospheric pressure** – Atmospheric pressure is the amount of force exerted by the weight of air in the Earth's atmosphere above an object. At sea level, atmospheric pressure is equal to 14.7 psi. If the dispensing gas is applied at 15 psi, then the absolute pressure on the beer is 29.7 psi (14.7 psi + 15 psi).

**Barrier tubing** – Plastic tubing with a lining of nylon or PET that provides a gas barrier to better protect the beer from oxidation.

**Beer line** – The tubing that is used to transport the beer from the keg to the faucet. It is also used to control the flow rate of beer by properly selecting the material and size of the beer line.

**Beer pump** – A mechanical pump that is generally driven by compressed air or $CO_2$ that can move beer great distances without changing the dissolved gases.

**Beer stone** – A mineral deposit of calcium oxalate that forms slowly on a surface from beer and is very difficult to remove.

**Caustic or Caustic Soda or NaOH – Sodium hydroxide** – A high pH chemical commonly blended into draught line cleaning solutions. Caustic will react with organic deposits in the draught beer line. Very effective, but also very dangerous. Commonly used in oven cleaners.

**Caustic potash or KOH or Potassium Hydroxide** – Similar to sodium hydroxide, but offers slightly different chemical properties in a blended cleaning solution.

**Check ball** – When the coupler is disconnected from the keg, this valve prevents beer from the beer line flowing out through the coupler.

**Check valve** – Also known as a Thomas Valve, this is the valve that allows $CO_2$ to flow into the keg but prevents beer from backing up into the gas line.

**Choker line** – Choker line, also known as restriction tubing, is a section of 3⁄16" internal diameter (ID) vinyl or flexible tubing of variable length installed at the tower end of a long-draw draught system.

**Cleaning Canister, Pressure Pot** – A canister for cleaning solution or rinse water that is connected to a pressure source pushing the solution through the lines like beer. Does not give sufficient velocity for mechanical cleaning, so this should only be used on short lines with longer chemical exposure.

**Coil-style jockey box** – A cooling system to bring beer to serving temperature at the point of dispense consisting of passing beer through a coil of stainless steel that is immersed in ice water. Often used at picnics or events where normal keg temperature cannot be maintained.

**Cold plate jockey box** – A cooling system to bring beer to serving temperature at the point of dispense consisting of a stainless steel coil embedded in an aluminum plate in contact with the ice. Cooling is the result of melting the ice rather than just heat transfer, so water must be drained away from the cold plate. Often used at picnics or events where normal keg temperature cannot be maintained.

**Coupler** – The connector from the draught system to the keg.

**Dewar** – An insulated, pressurized container for liquified gas such as $CO_2$.

**Direct-draw** – A draught beer system that has a short jumper connection from the keg to the faucet.

**Downtube** – see *spear*

**EDTA (ethylenediaminetetraacetic acid)** – A cleaning solution additive that can dissolve calcium mineral deposits in draught beer systems.

**Faucet** – The dispensing end of the draught beer system that controls the flow of beer.

**Flash chillers** – Mechanical cooling systems to bring beer to serving temperature at the point of dispense. Often used with flash-pasteurized kegs that can be stored at room temperature.

**FOB** – Foam on beer detector. A device that stops the flow of beer when the keg is empty before the beer line is filled with foam.

**Forced-air long-draw system** – A draught system where cold air from the walk-in cooler box is forced to the dispense tower, and then returned to the cooler. This forms a continuous air loop alongside beer hoses to keep them cold.

**Gas line** – The tubing that is used to bring $CO_2$ and other gases into the draught system. Vinyl gas line is used for pressures less than 50 psi; higher pressure will use braided gas line.

**Gauge pressure** – Gauge pressure is the pressure of the dispensing gas applied to beer beyond the local atmospheric pressure level, usually given as pounds per square inch, gauge (psig).

**Glycol** – see *propylene glycol*

**Glycol-cooled long-draw** – A draught system that uses a secondary refrigeration unit (power pack or glycol chiller) to maintain draught beer at the proper temperature all the way from the walk-in cooler to the faucet.

**Hand pump** – Often called a party pump or picnic pump, this is a manually operated pump that uses compressed air to dispense beer. This type of pump should only be used when the entire keg will be dispensed at one time, because oxygen will damage the beer.

**Ideal gauge pressure** – This is the setting on the regulator that you use when taking into consideration the $CO_2$ volumes of the beer, ABV, temperature, and altitude to calculate the pressure needed to maintain correct carbonation in the keg.

**ISBT** – International Society of Beverage Technologists, who created a quality standard for $CO_2$ for beverage use.

**Jockey box** – A cooler with a cooling coil or cold plate and faucets to chill the beer at the point of dispense.

**Jumper line** – The flexible piece of vinyl tubing used between the keg and draught beer system that should be replaced annually.

**Keg box/Kegerator** – A direct-draw, self-contained refrigerator where the number of kegs accommodated varies based on box and keg size.

**Kegs in a series** – Hooking multiple kegs together so the beer from the first flows through the second and then into the next so that the kegs can be changed less frequently.

**Lift** – The change in height from the keg to the faucet that is a component of system balance.

**Line** – Tubing that makes up the draught beer flow path.

**Long-draw** – A draught beer system over 50 feet long that uses barrier tubing in a refrigerated bundle that typically requires a mixed gas to avoid overcarbonation.

**$N_2$** – Diatomic nitrogen ($N_2$) is an inert gas that is used in a draught system to help propel beer a long distance. Specific beer styles uses nitrogen to enhance its head and mouthfeel of the beer.

**Nitrogen generator** – A system designed to separate nitrogen from compressed air, typically by membrane. Nitrogen used for beer dispense in a mixed gas application must be >99% pure.

**Party pump or picnic pump** – see *hand pump.*

**Polyethylene** – Stiffer tubing used in older refrigerated bundles. This oxygen-permeable material contributed to oxidation of the beer remaining in the lines and is now only recommended for use as glycol tubing.

**Potassium hydroxide (KOH)** – see *caustic potash*

**Propylene glycol** – A food-grade refrigerant that is recirculated through insulated tubing bundles to maintain beer temperature.

**psi** – Pounds per square inch. A unit of measure of gas pressure.

**psia** – Pounds per square inch, absolute. A measure of gas pressure against a perfect vacuum so it includes the atmospheric pressure of 14.7 psi at sea level.

**psig** – Pounds per square inch, gauge. A measure of gas pressure against the atmospheric pressure, typically seen on gas regulator gauges. Since atmospheric pressure varies with altitude, the gauge pressure must be adjusted with altitude.

**PVC – Polyvinyl Chloride** – Flexible tubing made from polyvinyl chloride (PVC) that is used for jumper line.

**Regulator** – A gas control valve that delivers a set gas pressure regardless of tank pressure. There may be a primary regulator on the gas source and a secondary regulator at the gas connection for each keg.

**Resistance** – A measure of the pressure drop across a component or over a length of tubing at the optimum beer flow rate.

**Rodding** – The use of small scrapers and steel rods to remove corrosion products.

**Sanitizer** – An EPA-registered product that is designed to kill microorganisms.

**Sankey** – The modern style of keg coupler. It is available in several versions to fit specific styles of keg valves produced in Europe and the U.S.

**Shank** – The connecting piece that goes through the cold box wall or tower and connects the tubing and tail piece to the tap. It also can help provide system pressure reduction.

**Sodium hydroxide (NaOH)** – see *caustic*

**Spear** – Also known as the "spear assembly" or "downtube." The spear is the component that allows $CO_2$ into the keg through vents and pushes beer up through the down tube and out of the keg

**Surfactants** – Compounds used in blended draught beer line cleaners that lower surface tension to enhance surface wetting, break the bond between deposits and the tubing surface, and suspend soils in cleaning solution so they can be removed.

**System balance** – Ensuring that the applied pressure matches the system requirements so that the beer dispenses at the optimum rate of about 2 fluid ounces per second, or 1 gallon per minute, while maintaining brewery specified carbonation level.

**Tail pieces** – The connectors that allow a piece of tubing to be attached to a piece of equipment.

**Tap** – see *coupler*

**Tavern head** – see *coupler*

**Tower** – The mount on the bar that holds the faucets and is cooled to maintain beer temperature up to the point of dispense.

**Trunk line** – Trunk line is the main section of tubing, usually barrier tubing, that runs the length of the system from the wall bracket in the cooler to the tower.

**Volumes of $CO_2$** – The concentration of $CO_2$ in beer expressed as volumes of gas at standard conditions per volume of beer.

**Walk-in cooler** – Enclosed refrigerated storage space that ideally maintains temperatures from 32–38°F to store beer and other food items. Dedicated beer storage is recommended to help control temperature. If you can walk into the storage space it is known as a walk-in-cooler.

**Water conditioners** – A component of a blended cleaner that is intended to carry away soils.

**Water stone** – A calcium carbonate mineral deposit that forms from water and can be removed with acid. ■

# INDEX

Entries in **boldface** refer to photos, illustrations and tables.